Dedication
To Ke Won Kang

Peter Kang is taking comments and questions at
kimchimanus@gmail.com.

Can't Stop Korean with K-pop

The Fun, Effective Way to Learn Korean

Peter Kang

ISBN-13: 978-1540898319

ISBN-10: 1540898318

Printed in USA by Createspace Publishing

Table of Contents

Introduction

K-pop has burst onto the world music scene as one of the bigger pop culture happenings of the 21st century. Though it has its early beginnings long before, it wasn't until the rise of the social network, web sites like Soompi, Allkpop and, of course, Youtube that it became a worldwide phenomenon. Korea, itself, has been on a remarkable run of economic, political, cultural evolution and has garnered much interest around the world. Unfortunately, some of this global interest has been dampened by the lack of lively materials to learn the Korean language. And what materials do exist are in the same tired vein of hagwon produced textbooks, rote learning, stodgy grammar books. This book is an attempt to remedy this dusty quandary- to add a fresh way of learning Korean.

This book is here to help you put in the rear view mirror the crusty belief that learning an East Asian language is difficult and harsh- like climbing Everest by yourself. While climbing Everest surely is difficult, dreary, heroic and relentlessly painful, learning Korean doesn't have to be.

With K-pop learning you can listen over and over with no problems of tedium. And you can improve your speaking ability by singing along at the desk, in the shower, going to the noraebang (song room). You will get vernacular Korean, entertaining lyrics, clear enunciation, everyday language- even if a quite a bit of it in the romantic parts of the language. Of course, while K-pop by itself will only teach a minority of the Korean, it does have its own knack for improving your pronunciation, phonics recognition, accustoming you to Korean syntax, lingo, rhythms of speech and the fundamentals of grammar.

Few activities combine enjoyment and language learning as songs do. The songs here are chosen for their pedagogical usefulness and because they are rather addictive songs. If you are beginning to learn Korean, start by making your way through the alphabet section and learning the phonics. Then learn the basic grammar. Then, use the songs in this book in anyway you desire and go thru the songs in any order. The notes and translation are provided to help you make sense of the lyrics. The goal is for the learner to be able to sing and understand the Korean free from any English. To help you get there, ride the energy and enthusiasm of K-pop and its endlessly repeatable listenability and sing-ability.

Peter Kang

The Korean Alphabet

The Korean Alphabet (한글) Pronunciation

The Korean alphabet consists of 24 letters with 14 consonants and 10 vowels. The 14 consonant letters are:

Consonants: ㄱ ㄴ ㄷ ㄹ ㅁ ㅂ ㅅ ㅇ ㅈ ㅊ ㅋ ㅌ ㅍ ㅎ
            g   n   d   l/f m   b   s   ng   j   ch   k   t   p   h

English sounds are represented by the letters under the Korean characters. Note that ㅇ is silent and is pronounced ng as the ending on syllables.

Vowels: ㅏ ㅓ ㅗ ㅜ ㅡ ㅣ ㅑ ㅕ ㅛ ㅠ
      a   eo   o   u   eu   I   ya   yeo yo yu

In addition there are compound letters - the digraphs.

5 double consonants: ㄲ ㄸ ㅃ ㅆ ㅉ
                  kk tt   pp ss jj

5 double vowels: ㅐ ㅒ ㅔ ㅖ ㅢ
             ae yae e   ye ui

6 vowels and diphthongs with a w: ㅘ ㅙ ㅚ ㅝ ㅞ ㅟ
                                wa wae oe wo we wi

The above English pronunciation analogs to the Korean alphabet are approximations and are only a loose guide. Preferably, the student should attempt to not use them at all beyond the introduction/memorization period to the Korean alphabet.
There are many good webpages with audios of Korean alphabet pronunciation. An excellent one is Wikibooks at https://en.wikibooks.org/wiki/Korean/Alphabet.

One of the keen features of Korean is the what-you-see-is-what-you-hear nature of Korean spelling. Unlike English which can have several pronunciations for a letter or two, Korean usually simply has one sound for one letter. This makes the learning of the phonics of Korean extremely simple and fast. You can be up and running with associations of sounds to letters in Korean with great accuracy in an hour or less.

The Korean Alphabet Scripting

Korean syllables are written with the pattern consonant+vowel, consonant+vowel+consonant, or consonant+vowel+consonant+consonant.

The vertically written vowels are to the right of the first consonant.

Example: ㄱ + ㅣ is written 기.

	ㅏ	ㅓ	ㅣ	ㅑ	ㅕ
ㄱ	가	나	기	갸	겨
ㄴ	나	너	니	냐	녀
ㄷ	다	더	디	댜	뎌
ㄹ	라	러	리	랴	려
ㅁ	마	머	미	먀	며
ㅂ	바	버	비	뱌	벼
ㅅ	사	서	시	샤	셔
ㅇ	아	어	이	야	여
ㅈ	자	저	지	쟈	져
ㅊ	차	처	치	챠	쳐
ㅋ	카	커	키	캬	켜
ㅌ	타	터	티	탸	텨
ㅂ	바	버	비	뱌	벼

The horizontally written vowels are under the first consonant.

Example: ㄱ + ㅡ is written 그.

	ㅗ	ㅜ	ㅡ	ㅛ	ㅠ
ㄱ	고	구	그	교	규
ㄴ	노	누	느	뇨	뉴
ㄷ	도	두	드	됴	듀
ㄹ	로	루	르	료	류
ㅁ	모	무	므	묘	뮤
ㅂ	보	부	브	뵤	뷰
ㅅ	소	수	스	쇼	슈
ㅇ	오	우	으	요	유
ㅈ	조	주	즈	죠	쥬
ㅊ	초	추	츠	쵸	츄
ㅋ	코	쿠	크	쿄	큐
ㅌ	토	투	트	툐	튜
ㅂ	보	부	브	뵤	뷰

When a third letter is added to the syllable, it is under the previous two letters.

Example: ㄱ + ㅏ + ㅁ is written 감, ㄱ + ㅗ + ㅁ is written 곰.

The fourth letter is written to the right of the bottom consonant.

Example: ㄱ + ㅏ + ㅂ + ㅅ is written 값. ㄱ + ㅡ + ㄹ + ㅁ is written 긂.

Korean Basic Grammar

Korean is an agglutinative language, meaning the verb endings show tense, voice and formality.
The syntax is S-O-V. Subject-Object-Verb. This takes some adjusting to for English speakers and music is an excellent way to get accustomed to this difference.

Korean Tenses

The vast majority of K-Pop songs are written in the present tense and in the informal language. Korean has several layers of formal language. We will consider only the most common casual and formal styles.

The Present Tense

The dictionary verb is written with ~다.

Example: 가다 (to go), 오다 (to go), 가르치다 (to teach), 살다 (to live)

The most common formal present tense uses ~어요/아요 endings. Koreans will use this ending when talking to a stranger or an older person.
Verb stems ending with vowels ㅗ or ㅏ are followed by 아요.

Verb stems ending with vowels other than ㅗ or ㅏ are followed by 어요.

Drop the 다 to leave the stem and add the appropriate tense ending:

> 가다 -> 가 + 요 -> 가요 - go
>
> 있다 -> 있 + 어요 -> 있어요 - am/is/are
>
> 먹다 -> 먹 + 어요 -> 먹어요 - eat
>
> 마시다 -> 마시 + 어요 -> 마셔요 - drink

Note that 하다 (to do) changes to 해요.

The informal present ending uses ~어/여 or will simply drop 다 and the simple base verb will end the statement:

> 난 먹어. - I eat.
>
> 읽어 - read

K-Pop Example (Girls' Generation Express 999):

> 더 강한 커피가 필요해.
> ...need a stronger coffee.

The ending is informal present. The verb is 필요하다 meaning "to need". 다 is dropped. 하 from 하다 (to do) becomes 해. The formal ending would have been written 필요해요.

The Past Tense

The most common formal past tense endings are 았어요/었어요/였어요. These are added to the verb stem. It's basically adding -ㅆ어요.
Verb stems ending with vowels ㅗ or ㅏ are followed by 았어요.
Verb stems ending with vowels other than ㅗ or ㅏ are followed by 었어요.
Verb stem 하 is followed by 였어요:

> 사다 - to buy. Verb stem 사
> 사 + 았어요 -> 샀어요 - bought
> 오다 - to come. Verb stem 오
> 오 + 았어요 -> 왔어요 - came
> 적다 - to write down. Verb stem 적
> 적 + 었어요 -> 적었어요 (wrote)
> 하다 (to do). Verb stem 하
> 하 + 였어요 becomes 했어요 (did)

K-Pop Example (Girls' Generation Express 999):

> 선생님이 모자를 쓴 채 학교에 들어갔어요.
> The teacher went to school while wearing a hat.

The Future Tense

A standard future tense in Korean adds ~ㄹ/을 거예요, which means "will" or "be going to".

Verb + ㄹ/을 거예요

> 1. Verb stems ending with a vowel (보다, 가다, 자다) add ㄹ 거예요.
> 2. Verb stems ending with a consonant (먹다, 찾다, 붙다) add 을 거예요.
> 3. Verb stems already ending with ㄹ at the end (놀다, 멀다, 살다) just add 거예요.

Examples:

가다 - to go

가 + ㄹ 거예요 -> 갈 거예요 - will go

...지금 갈 거예요. - ...am/is/are going to go now.

...혼자 갈 거예요. - ...am/is/are going to go alone.

하다 - to do

하 + ㄹ 거예요. -> 할 거예요. - will do

...뭐 할 거예요? - What am/is/are ...going to do?

...언제 할 거예요? - When am/is/are ...going to do?

입다 - to wear

입 + 을 거예요 -> 입을 거예요. - will wear

...청바지 입을 거예요. - ...am/is/are going to wear blue jeans.

...티셔츠 입을 거예요. - ...am/is/are going to wear a t-shirt.

Subject and Object Particles

Subject Particles ~는 / 은 and ~가 / 이

는/은 and 가/이 both are used as a subject marker.
는 and 가 are attached to words ending in vowels:

바다 + 는 -> 바다는 - the sea

바다 + 가 -> 바다가 - the sea

그녀 + 는 -> 그녀는 - the girl

그녀 + 가 -> 그녀가 - the girl

은 and 이 are attached to words ending in consonants:

밥 + 은 -> 밥은 - the rice

밥 + 이 -> 밥이 - the rice

책 + 은 -> 책은 - the book

책 + 이 -> 책이 - the book

However, 는/은 introduces a topic or a subject whereas 가/이 identifies a subject. The topic particle, 는/은, is used in cases when we make a general or factual statement whereas 가/이 is not.

Example:

> 비행기는 빠르다. - Planes are fast.

However, if you are a passenger in a plane and you are talking about your own plane compared to say faster planes, you might say:

비행기가 느리다 - (My) plane is slow.

So the identifier particle, 가/이, indicates a specific person or thing that the speaker and listener know or are aware of. In the example above, it is the plane that I am riding.

Another example:

> 바다는 푸르다. - The sea is blue. (A general statement)

However, suppose you see the sea at night and you may effuse:

> 바다가 까맣다! - The sea is black! (A particular statement)

K-Pop Example (2NE I Am The Best):

> 내가 제일 잘 나가. - I am the best.

내 + 가 = 내가 - I. I is the particular I. Don't confuse first 가 the second with the second 가. The second 가 is part of verb 나가 meaning "to go out".

Object Particles ~을/를

을 is used after a noun ending in a consonant:

> 옷 + 을 -> 옷을 - clothes

를 is used after a noun ending in a vowel.

> 사과 + 를 -> 사과를 - apple

Object words in Korean function similarly to object words in English:

...책을 읽었어요. - ...read a book.

...강을 건넜어요. - ...crossed a river.

K-Pop Example (2NE1 I Am The Best):

가치를 논하자면... - If...talking about my value...

가치를 - value

를 marks 가치 as the object. As the thing we are talking about.

Korean Syntax

The Korean language follows different structures and word orders than English. The big difference is that the verb always comes at the end of the Korean sentence, unlike in English. The following are the four basic Korean sentence structures.

Note the abbreviations used in the explanation and the course of this book:

S-subject, N-noun, V-verb, A-adjective, O-object

1. S + N + V(to be).

   나는 학생이다. - I am a student.

   나는 - I, 학생 - student, 이다 - am

2. S + V. Subject + Verb

   채영은 달린다. - Chae Young runs. (Chae Young- S, runs- V)

   채영- Chae Young (a name)

   은 (topic marker for Chae Young)

   달린다 – run

3. S + A + V.

   그는 정말 멍청해. - He is very stupid.

   그는 – He

   정말- very

   멍청해 – stupid (literal English "does stupid")

   채영은 정말 예쁘다. – Chae Young is very beautiful.

   예쁘다 – beautiful

4. S + O + V. Subject + Object + Verb

   나는 물을 마신다. – I drink water.

   나는 – I

   물을 – water

   마신다 – drink

Common Words, Particles, and Their Usage

~이다- "to be"
Verbs typically appear at the end of the sentence or clause.
~이다 is the base form and combines with a noun.

1. 열쇠입니다.   It's a key.
2. 사랑입니다.   It's love.
3. 사과입니다.   It's an apple.

~이에요, ~예요- "to be"
~이에요, ~예요 are the polite forms of ~이다. ~이에요 follows a consonant. ~예요 follows a vowel.

1. 밥이에요.   It's rice.
2. 코예요.   It's a nose.
3. 사과예요.   It's an apple.

아닙니다/아니에요- "it isn't"
Noun + 이/가 아닙니다

1. 상추는 과일이 아닙니다.   Lettuce is not fruit.
2. 의사는 변호사가 아니에요.   The doctor is not a lawyer.
3. 그는 가수가 아닙니다.   He is not a singer.

Descriptive verb + 요- "it's..."
요 is formal ending of the verb and used with strangers, older persons.

1. 맛있어요.   It's delicious.
2. 나빠요.   It's bad.
3. 좋아요   It's good.

이것- "this one", 그것- "that one", 저것- "that one"
이것- "this, this one"

1. 이것은 비싸요.   This is expensive.

그것- "that, that one"

    1. 그것 은 약이예요.   That's medicine.

저것- "that / that one over there (used for farther things)"

    1. 저것은 은행이예요.   That's a bank.

못 + verb- "can not…"

못 is a negative preceding an action verb.

    1. 요즘은 잘 못 자요.   Lately I can't sleep well.
    2. 나는 술을 못 마셔요.   I can't drink (alcohol)

~마다 – "every"

~마다 is used nouns and translates to "every…"

    1. 부산 가는 버스는 한 시간마다 있어요.
There is bus ever hour that goes to Busan.
    2. 날마다 수영합이다.   I swim everyday.
    3. 게마다 성격을 달라료.   Each dog's personality is different.

~의 (possessive marker)

The possession marker 의 follows a word to make it possessive.

    1. 어머니의 전화기.   Mother's phone.
    2. 유리의 자동차.   Yuri's car.
    3. 저의 남자친구가 스물 살이에요. My boyfriend is twenty years old.

~에- "to, from, at, in, on"

~에 is often used with verbs like 가다, 오다, 도착하다, 돌아가다, 내려가다, 올라가다. It shows the direction in which an action proceeds. In English, it would be the same as "to/from".

    1. 날마다 학교에 가요.   Every day I go to school
    2. 화장실에 갔다 왔어요.   I went came back from the bathroom

The second basic meaning of this particle is when it is used with 있다 or 없다, when used with these it expresses the location of a person or thing. In English, it would be "in" or "on".

1. 소파 위에 동생이 있어요.   My brother is on the sofa.
2. 가족들은 저 동굴에 있어요.   My family is in that cave

것- "thing"

Although 것 can be translated as "thing", it is often not said in the English translation, despite it being a very important part of the grammar.

1. 누구의 것이에요?   Whose thing is this? / Whose is it?
2. 이 음식은 누구의 것이에요?   Whose is this food?

In spoken Korean 의 is often removed.

1. 이 연필은 선생님 것입니까?   Is this the teacher's pencil?

많다- "a lot, many"

1. 많아요. (sounds like 마나요)   There is a lot.
2. 숙제가 많아요.   (I have) a lot of homework.
3. 친구는 숙제가 많아요.   My friend has a lot of homework.

The "I have" isn't actually said in Korean, but it is implied based on context.

없다- "to not exist, to not have"

없다 has the opposite meaning of 있다.

1. 김밥이 없어요.   There isn't / I don't have gimbap.
2. 저는 여동생이 없어요   I don't have a younger sister.
3. 제 가방이 없어요.   My bag isn't there.

Other prepositions or location markers.

위- "above, on top, up"

1. 책상 위에 고양이가 있어요.   There is a cat on top of the desk.

밑- " below, under, down"

    1. 책상 밑에 쥐가 있어요.   There is a mouse under the desk.

속 / 안- "inside, in"

    1. 책상 속에 펭귄이 있어요.   There is a penguin in the desk.

옆- "side, next to"

    1. 책상 옆에 곰이 있어요.   There is a bear next to the desk.

앞- "in front of"

    1. 책상 앞에 하마가 있어요.   There is a hippo in front of the desk.

뒤- "behind"

    1. 책상 뒤에 기린이 있어요.   There is a giraffe behind my desk.

Ways to say "very" in Korean

너무- "very, too much"

    1. 이 책은 너무 좋아요!   This book is very good!

매우- "very (mostly written only)"

    1. 이 라면은 너무 맛있어요!   This ramen is very delicious!

아주- "very, quite"

    1. 이 책은 아주 비싸요!   This book is too expensive!

(object) 을/를 주세요- "please give, please"

    1. 귤을 주세요.   A tangerine please.
    2. 차를 주세요.   Some tea please.
    3. 커피 주세요.   Coffee please.

~와/~과- "and"

와 and 과 are used to connect nouns in a list. 와 is used after vowels, 과 is used after consonants.

1. 차와 커피를 주세요.   A tea and a coffee please.
2. 고양이와 강아지가 귀여워요.   Cats and puppies are cute.
3. 제 어머니와 아버지는 너무 착해요.   My mother and father are really kind.
4. 김밥과 국과 바나나를 주세요.   Give me gimbap, soup, and a banana.

~과/와 and ~랑/이랑 and ~하고- "with"

과/와 is most commonly used in writing.

1. 저는 남자친구와 함께 커피를 마시러 커피숍에 갔어요.
I went with my boyfriend to a coffee shop to drink coffee.

랑/이랑 is most commonly used in speech and tends to be more informal

1. 저는 밥이랑 빵 먹는 것을 좋아해요.
I like eating rice and bread.

하고 is most commonly used in writing and tends to be more formal

1. 오늘 강남하고 신사에 갔습니다.
I went to Gangnam and Sinsa today.

~고- "and" or "then"

Used to express two or more actions, states, or facts.

1. 저 학교는 커고 학교의 교실도 커요.
That school is big and the classrooms are also big.
2. 저의 여자 친구는 귀엽고 예뻐요.
My girlfriend is cute and pretty
3. 저는 자고 한국어를 공부했어요.
I slept then studied Korean.
4. 우리는 사과를 먹고 바나나를 먹자.
Let's eat the apple and then eat the banana.

~도- "also, too, again, even"

1. 너도 거기 있었니?
Were you there also?
2. 아버지는 키가 커요. 그리고 저도 키가 커요.
My farther is tall. Also, I am tall too.
3. 텀은 한국말 잘 해요. 그런데 캐트도 잘 해요.
Tom speaks Korean well. Kate too speaks well.

Past tense for 이다 and 아니다

이다 (it is, I am, he is, she is etc.) and 아니다 (it isn't, I am not, he isn't, she isn't etc.) can be conjugated into the past tense as shown:

Verb	Past tense (after consonant)	Past tense (after consonant)
이다	이었어요	였어요
아니다	아니었어요	아니었어요

1. 전 원이었어요.   It was 1000 won.
2. 삼만 원이었어요.   It was 30,000 won.
3. 언제 였어요?   When was it?
4. 어제가 아니었어요. 토요일이었어요.
It wasn't yesterday. It was Saturday.

~지 마세요/~ 지 말고- "do no..."

1. 가지마세요.   Please do not go
2. 보지마세요.   Please do not look
3. 오늘은 눈을 많이 내려서 일로 차를 타지 마.
Today lots of snow is coming down, so do not drive
4. 오늘 만나지 말고 다음에 만나.   Let's not meet today, lets meet next time.

Verb + 고 싶다- "hope to..., wish to..., want to..."

1. 너는 나를 보고 싶어?   Do you want to see me/ Do you miss me?
2. 가족을 보고 싶다   I want to see my family/ I miss my family.

3. 화장실에 가고 싶어요	I want to go to the bathroom.
4. 고기를 먹고 싶다	I wish to eat meat.

~한테, ~에게- "to"

에게 is used more for writing. 한테 is used more often when speaking.

1. 새한테 먹을 것을 주었다.	I gave birds something to eat.
2. 남자친구한테 떡을 줄 거예요.	I will give rice cakes to my boyfriend.
3. 제 아버지에게 선물을 줬어요.	I gave a present to my father.
4. 선생님에게 사과를 줬어요.	I gave an apple to my teacher.

~한테서, ~에게서- "from"

에게서 is used more for written Korean. 한테서 is used more commonly when speaking.

1. 저는 여자친구한테서 메시지를 받았어요.
I received a message from my girlfriend.
2. 누구한테서 이 선물을 받았어요?
Who did you get this present from?
3. 제 아버지에게서 선물을 받았어요.
I received a present from my father.
4. 선생님에게서 사과를 받았어요.
I received an apple from my teacher.

Verb + 아/어/여 보다- "try, see…"
Conjugation rules:

가다 → 가 봐요

먹다 → 먹어 봐요 (add 어 after consonant)

1. 한번 마셔 보세요.	Please try this one time (drink).
2. 입어 보세요.	Please try this on.
3. 그 책 읽어 봤어?	Have you (ever) read that book?
4. 잘 생각해 보세요.	Please try to think about it.

~ㄹ/을 때- "when..."

1. 저녁을 먹을 때 손님이 오셨어요.
When I was eating dinner, a visitor came.
2. 공원에 도착했을 때는 아침이었어요.
When we arrived at the park, it was morning.
3. 바쁘지 않을 때 전화해.
When you aren't busy, call me.
4. 저는 돈을 받을 때 행복할 거예요.
When I receive (the) money, I will be happy

Basic command form.
The basic command form drops the 요 ending for the verb.

1. 가!	Go!
2. 마셔!	Drink!
3. 해 봐!	Try to do it!
4. 줘!	Give!
5. 앉어	Sit!

Verb + 지 않다- "to not..."

1. 한국어는 어렵지 않아요.	Korean is not difficult.
2. 내일 가지 않아요.	I won't go tomorrow.
3. 가지 않았어요.	I didn't go.
4. 저는 행복하지 않아요	I am not happy
5. 춥지 않을 거예요.	It won't be cold.

Verb + ㄹ까- "shall..."

1. 몇 시에 갈까요?	What time shall we go?
2. 누구한테 전화할까?	Who shall I call?
3. 몇 분 수영할까요?	How many minutes shall we swim?
4. 오늘 음식을 요리할까요?	Shall we cook some food today?
5. 도사관에 갈까요?	Shall we go to the library?

~에 대해- "about…"

1. 나는 너에 대해 생각했어.   I thought about you
2. 나는 나의 아버지에 대해 말했어.   I spoke about my father
3. 그 영화에 대해 몰랐어요.   I didn't know about that movie.
4. 네 여자친구에 대해 알아요.   I know about your girlfriend.
5. 이 책에 대해 알아요?   Do you know about this book?

~부터…~까지- "from…to…"

1. 서울부터 부산까지   from Seoul to Pusan
2. 집부터 학교까지   from home to school
3. 시에서 4 시까지는 집에 있을 거예요.   I will be at home from 1 to 4.
4. 2012 년부터 2014 년까지 미국에 있었어요.
I was in US from 2012 to 2014.

Verb + ㄹ/을 수(가) 있다 and Verb + ㄹ/을 수(가) 없다 – "can do…" and "can't do…"

1. 네, 할 수 있죠.   Yes, I can do that.
2. 수영할 수 있어요?   Can you swim?
3. 5 시부터 시작할 수 없었어요.   I couldn't start at 5 o'clock.
4. 조용한 소리를 들을 수가 없어요.   I can't hear quiet sounds.

~(으)로- "by, through"

1. 노트 필기는 펜으로 해주세요.   Please take notes with a pen.
2. 컴퓨터는 물로 씻으면 안 된다.   A computer should not be washed with water.
3. 택시로 갈 거예요.   I will go by taxi.
4. 이메일로 보냈어요.   I sent it by email.
5. 카드로 샀어요.   I bought it with my credit card.

Noun + 이/가 되다- "to become…"

The conjugated form of 되어 can be contracted to 돼.

For verbs, you must use: V + 게 되다

1. 나는 배우가 되고 싶어요.   I want to become an actor.
2. 나는 선생님이 될 거예요.   I'm going to become a teacher.
3. 저의 아들은 20 살이 되었어요.   My son became(turned) twenty.
4. 우리는 친구가 되었어요.   We became friends.
5. 저는 어릴 때 고아가 되었어요.   I was orphaned when I was child.

Verb + 고 있다- "...ing"
This is the continuous form the verb.

1. 아이들은 먹고 있어요.
The children are eating.
2. 제 친구들이 기차를 타고 있어요.
My friends are riding the train.
3. 지금 누나하고 티비를 보고 있어요.
Right now, I am watching TV with my older sister.
4. 넷 시까지 일하고 있었어요.
I was working until 4:00.

Past tense examples.

1. 제 여자친구는 할아버지의 노트북을 쓰고 있어요.
My girlfriend is using my grandfather's laptop computer.
2. 지금 친구들이랑 맛있는 것을 먹고 있어요.
Right now, I am eating delicious things with my friends.

Verb + (으)려면...- "if (verb) then....)
This pattern is equivalent to if the subject intends to (verb) then a consequence.

1. 경복궁에 가려면 어디로 가야 하나요?
How can I get to Kyoung Bok Palace?
2. 돈을 벌려면 일을 해야 합니다.
If you want to earn money, you must work.
3. 통장을 만들려면 신분증이 필요해요.
If you intend to open an account, you need your ID card.
4. 한국말을 잘 하려면 어떻게 해야 할까요?
What should I do to speak good Korean?
5. 철수씨를 만나려면 사무실로 가 보세요.
If you want to meet Chul Su, go to his office.

Adjective + 군요, Verb + 는군요, Noun + (이)군요

This form expresses surprise or wonder.

1. 어! 눈이 참 많이 오는군요!   Oh! It's really snowing a lot!
2. 김치를 좋아하는군요!   You really like kimchi!
3. 강아지가 정말 귀엽군요!   Your puppy is really cute!

어느- "which", 무슨- "what", 어떤- "what kind of"

Each of these words require a noun following them.

1. 무슨 차를 좋아해요?   What tea do you like?
2. 무슨 책을 싫어해요?   What book do you dislike?
3. 어느 나라 사람이세요?   Which country are you from?
4. 어느 식당 피자가 맛있어요?   Which restaurant's pizza is delicious?
5. 철수가 어떤 사람이에요?   What kind of person is Chul-soo?
6. 어떤 게 나을까?   Which one would be better?

하지만 – "but, however"; 그리고- "and then"; 그래서- "so, therefore, that's why"

These connectors are typically used between sentences not just words.

1. 배불러요. 하지만 더 먹고 싶어요.
I am full. But I want to eat more.
2. 일월에 처음으로 한국에 갔어요. 그리고, 중국에도 갔어요.
I went to Korea for the first time in January. And then I went to China too.
3. 최근 별로 공부하지 않았어요. 그래서 제 성적이 안 좋아요.
Recently I haven't studied much. That's why my grades aren't good.

EXO- Overdose

Baekhyun, Chan Yeol, Xuimin, Suho, Zhang, DO, Kai
Lu Han, Tao

Lyrics/Translation/Notes

모든 걸 걸고 널 들이킨 나
I drew you in closer with all I had
모든- all; 걸- thing; 걸다- to risk, hang, bet; 들이키다- to close, bring in, take

이젠 돌이킬 수도 없다
Now I can't turn it back
돌이키다- to return

이건 분명 위험한 중독
This is clearly a dangerous addiction
분명- certainly, clearly; 위험- danger; ~한- (adjective marker); 중독- addiction

So bad, no one can stop her.
Her Love Her Love,
Her love her love
오직 그것만 바라 그녀의 사랑 하나뿐인걸
The only thing I want is her love
오직- only; 바라- want, desire; 하나- one; ~뿐- only

치명적인 Fantasy
Her fatal fantasy

황홀함 그 안에 취해
I'm drunk with ecstasy

황홀함- ecstasy; ~함- (noun marker, similar to "-ness"); 취해- to be drunk

Oh, She wants me.
Oh, She's got me.
Oh, She hurts me. Oh, she wants me~ Oh, she's got me, Oh, she hurts me
좋아, 더욱 갈망하고 있어
What else can be better than this? (lit. Good, there's more craving)
더욱- more; 갈망- craving; ~하고 있다- ...ing (continuous verb ending)

Someone Call the Doctor.
날 붙잡고 말해줘
Hold me and tell me (lit. Hold me and give talk)
붙잡다- hold; V+줘- ...give
사랑은 병, 중독 Overdose
Love is a sickness, an addiction, overdose
병- sickness, illness; 중독- overdose
시간이 지날수록 통제는 힘들어져
It's harder to control as time goes by
지날-pass; +수록-as; 통제- control; 힘들어(져)- difficult(becomes)
점점 깊숙이 빠져간다
Eh-oh I'm falling deeper into her
점점- bit by bit; 깊숙- depth; 빠져- fall into; 간다/가다- to go

Too Much, 너야.
Your love, 이건 Overdose.
Oh, too much, it's you, your love, this is overdose
Too Much, 너야.
Your love, 이건 Overdose.
Too much, it's you, your love, this is overdose

놀리는 그 손길로 온 너
The teasing way you came
놀리- play; 손- hand; 길- way
본능은 너를 갈구해 좀 더
My instinct desires you more
본능- instinct; 갈구하다- to desire, strive
가빠진 숨으로 질식된 후에
After my breath quickens and chokes
가빠진- to suck; 질식- suffocation; ~된- became
전율, 그리곤 한숨
I feel a shiver and then a sigh

전율- shiver; 그리곤- and; 한숨- sigh

<u>Her Love Her Love,</u>
<u>독한 약 같아 내겐.</u>
is like strong medicine to me
독- poison; 내겐- to me
<u>헤어나올 수 없는 Destiny</u>
Destiny I can't escape
헤어나올- separate, split
<u>피는 뜨거워졌지</u>
My blood gets hotter
뜨거워- hot; 졌지- become
<u>마침내 모두 지배해.</u>
and eventually controls all of me
마침내- in the end; 지배해- to be lost, dominated

<u>Oh, She wants me.</u>
<u>Oh, She's got me.</u>
<u>Oh, She hurts me.</u>
<u>계속 너만 그리고 그린 나</u>
I keep thinking and thinking about you
계속- continually; 너- you; 만- only; 그리다- to miss, long for

<u>Someone Call the Doctor.</u>
<u>날 붙잡고 말해줘</u>
hold me and tell me
<u>사랑은 병, 중독 Overdose</u>
Love is a sickness, an addiction, overdose
<u>시간이 지날수록 통제는 힘들어져</u>
It's harder to control as time goes by
<u>점점 깊숙이 빠져간다 Eh-oh</u>
I'm falling deeper into her

<u>Too Much, 너야.</u>
Too much, it's you,
<u>Your love, 이건 Overdose.</u>
your love, this is overdose
<u>Too Much, 너야.</u>
Too much, it's you,
<u>Your love, 이건 Overdose.</u>
your love, this is overdose

모두 다 내게 물어봐
Everyone asks me
내- me; -게- to; 물어봐- ask and see

내가 변한 것 같대
if I've changed
변한- changed; 것 같대- seems like

심장에 네가 박혀버린 듯
It's like you're nailed into my heart
심장- heart; ~에- to; 박혀- nailed; 버린- lost, wasted

세상이 온통 너인데.
My world is filled with you
세상- world; 온통- full, completely; 인데- it is

멈출 수 없어 이미 가득한 널
I can't stop, I'm already filled with you
멈추다- to stop; ~수 없어- can't; 가득한- full

지금 이 순간, You're in my heart
Right now, this moment, you're in my heart

E.X.O

난 너를 맛보고 너를 마신다
I taste you and drink you
맛보고- try taste; 마신다- to drink

온 몸이 떨려와.
My whole body trembles
몸- body; 떨리다- to tremble; V+와- ...come

계속 들이켜도 아직 모자라.
I keep drinking you in but it's not enough yet
들이켜도- keep taking in; 모자라- not enough

손끝까지 전율시킨 갈증
This thirst sends shivers even to my fingertips,
손끝- fingertips; -까지- to; 전율- shiver; 시킨- ordered; 갈증- thirst

이 순간을 잡아.
hold onto that moment
순간- moment; 잡아- grab; hold

질주를 멈추지 마 너무 좋아,
Don't stop going, it's so good,
질주- striving; 멈추다- to stop; 너무- to, so

I can't stop.
Hey Doctor!

지금 이대로 괜찮나 나?
am I okay like this?
이대로- like this; ~로- thru; 괜찮나- okay?

주체할 수 없는
It is uncontrollable
주체- control

이끌림 속에 녹아내려가 난
Melting down in this attraction
이끌림- attraction; 녹다- to melt; 내려가- descend

이 느낌 없이는 죽은 거나 마찬가진걸
Without this feeling, it's like I am dead
느낌- feeling; 없다- to be without; 죽은- dead; 거나/건- thing; 마찬가진- right, match

내가 사는 이유,
The reason I live is
사는- living; 이유- reason

난 너란 달콤함에 중독
my addiction to sweetness of you
~란- with; 달콤함- sweetness

Someone call the doctor!
난 그녀가 필요해
I need her
그녀- that girl; 필요하다- to need

하루도 난 버틸 수 없어 (버티지 못해)
I can't stand it for a single day (can't last)
버티다- to endure

벗어나고 싶지 않은 천국 같은 너
You're like heaven that I don't want to leave.
벗어나다- to take off, undress; 싶다- to want, to desire; 천국- heaven

긴 긴 이 덫은 아름다워. Eh oh
This long trap is wonderful.
긴- long; 덫- trap; 아름다워- beautiful

Too Much, 너야.
Too much, it's you,
Your love, 이건 Overdose.
your love, this is overdose

32

Too Much, 너야.
Too much, it's you,
Your love, 이건 Overdose.
your love, this is overdose

Twice- Cheer Up

Lyrics/Translation/Notes

매일 울리는 벨벨벨
Every day ringing, the bell bell bell
매일- every day; 울리는- ringing

이젠 나를 배려 해줘
Now care for me
이젠- now; 배려- consider, care for; 해줘- do give

배터리 낭비하긴 싫어
I don't wanna waste my battery
배터리- battery; 낭비하다- to waste; 싫어- don't like

자꾸만 와 자꾸 자꾸만 와
It keeps coming, it keeps coming
자꾸- often; 와- come

전화가 펑 터질 것만 같아
Like my phone's gonna explode
전화- phone; 펑- boom; 터질- will explode; 것만 같아- only seems

몰라 몰라 숨도 못 쉰대 I don't know,

I don't know, he says he can't even breathe

숨- breathe, 쉬다- to breathe, ~은/는대- in the case of

나 때문에 힘들어

He says he's struggling because of me

힘들어- hard, difficult

쿵 심장이 떨어진대 왜

He says his heart is dropping hard, why?

쿵- wham, bump; 떨어진다/떨어지는- dropping

걔 말은 나 너무 예쁘대

He says that I'm so pretty

걔- that guy/girl (usually spoken); 예쁘다- to be pretty; ~대- it is

자랑 하는건 아니구

I'm not showing off or anything

자랑- boast; V+구/고- ...and (고 is standard, 구 is spoken dialect in Seoul area)

아 아까는 못 받아서 미안해

Sorry I couldn't pick up earlier

아까는- before; 받다- to receive; ~아서- since; 미안해- sorry

친구를 만나느라 shy shy shy

I was meeting my friends, shy shy shy

만나다- to meet; V+느라- 1. while 2. because

만나긴 좀 그렇구 미안해

I can't really meet you right now, sorry

좀 있다 연락할게 later

I'll call you a little later

좀- little; 연락- call, ~할게- will

조르지마 얼마 가지 않아

Don't beg, then you won't last long

조르다- to beg; 얼마- how much

부르게 해줄게 Baby

I'll let you call me baby

부르다- to call

아직은 좀 일러 내 맘 같긴 일러

It's still a little too early, too early for my heart

아직은- still; 일러- early

하지만 더 보여줄래

to feel the same – But I'll show you more

하지만- but; 더- more; 보여주다- to show; V+ㄹ/을래- (expresses the will or Intention of the speaker)

CHEER UP BABY CHEER UP BABY

좀 더 힘을 내 Cheer up a little more

Show little more strength Cheer up a little more

힘- strength; 내- give, show

여자가 쉽게 맘을 주면 안돼

A girl can't give her heart too easily

여자- girl; 쉽게- easily; 맘- heart; 주다- to give; -면- if; 안- not; 돼- right

그래야 니가 날 더 좋아하게 될걸

That's how you'll get to like me even more

그래- that; ~야- should; 더- more; ~하게- (adjective marker)

태연하게 연기할래 아무렇지 않게

I'll act calm, as if it's nothing

태연- calm; ~하게- ~ly; 연기- act; 아무렇지- whatever

내가 널 좋아하는 맘 모르게

So, you won't know that I like you

모르게- unknowingly

Just get it together

And then baby CHEER UP

안절부절 목소리가 여기까지 들려

I can hear the anxiety in your voice

안절부절- anxiety; 목소리- voice; 여기까지- to here; 들려- hear

땀에 젖은 전화기가 여기서도 보여

I can see the sweat forming on your phone

땀- sweat; ~에- from; 젖은- wetted; 전화기- phone; 여기서도- even from here

바로 바로 대답하는 것도 매력 없어

It's not attractive to answer right away

바로- immediately; 대답- answer; 매력- attraction

메시지만 읽고 확인 안 하는 건 기본

Only reading your text and not responding is a given

메시지- message; 읽다- to read; 확인- confirmation; 기본- a given

어어어 너무 심했나 boy

Oops, was I too harsh boy?

너무- too; 심했나- was harsh

이러다가 지칠까 봐 걱정되긴 하고
I'm worried that you'll get tired
지칠- fatigue; 걱정- worry

어어어 안 그러면 내가 더
But if not, I'll more
안- not; 그러면- if not that

빠질 것만 같어 빠질 것만 같어
fall you. I think I'll fall for you.
빠지다- to fall for

아 답장을 못해줘서 미안해
Sorry I couldn't respond
답장- response; 못해- can't; V+서- because...; 미안해- sorry

친구를 만나느라 shy shy shy
I was meeting my friends, shy shy shy
친구- friend; 만나다- to meet

만나긴 좀 그렇구 미안해
I can't really meet you right now, sorry

좀 있다 연락할게 later
I'll call you a little later
연락- call; 할게- will do

조르지마 어디 가지 않아
Don't beg, I'm not going anywhere
어디- where, anywhere

되어줄게 너의 Baby
I'll be your baby
줄게- will give

너무 빨린 싫어 성의를 더 보여
But not too fast, show me you mean it
빨린- fast; 성의- genuineness

내가 널 기다려줄게
I'll wait for you, okay.
기다리다- to wait; V+ㄹ/을게- (permission tag as in "if it's okay")

CHEER UP BABY CHEER UP BABY
좀 더 힘을 내 Cheer up a little more
Show little more strength Cheer up a little more
여자가 쉽게 맘을 주면 안돼
A girl can't give her heart too easily

37

그래야 니가 날 더 좋아하게 될걸
That's how you'll get to like me even more
태연하게 연기할래 아무렇지 않게
I'll act calm, as if it's nothing
내가 널 좋아하는 맘 모르게
So, you won't know that I like you
Just get it together
And then baby CHEER UP

나도 니가 좋아 상처 입을까 봐
I like you too, I'm just worried I'll get hurt
상처- injury, hurt
걱정되지만 여자니까 이해해주길
I hope you understand because I'm a girl
속 마음 들킬 까봐 겁이나
I'm scared that you'll find out how I feel
속- inside, in; 겁이나- become fearful
지금처럼 조금만 더 다가와
Come to me little by little just like now
지금- now; ~처럼- like, as; 조금- little; 다가와- come
그리 오래 걸리진 않아
It won't take that long
그리- somewhat; 오래- long time; 걸리다- to take
Just get it together
And then baby CHEER UP
Be a man, a real man
Gotta see u love me
Like a real man
Be a man, a real man
Gotta see u love me
Like a real man

CHEER UP BABY CHEER UP BABY
좀 더 힘을 내 Cheer up a little more
Show little more strength Cheer up a little more
여자가 쉽게 맘을 주면 안돼
A girl can't give her heart too easily
그래야 니가 날 더 좋아하게 될걸
That's how you'll get to like me even more
태연하게 연기할래 아무렇지 않게
I'll act calm, as if it's nothing
내가 널 좋아하는 맘 모르게
So, you won't know that I like you

Just get it together
And then baby CHEER UP

Twice- TT

Momo, Mina, Jeongyeon, Chaeyoung, Dahyun, Sana, Jihyo, Nayeon, Tzuyu

Lyrics/Translation/Notes

이러지도 못하는데
I can't stand this
이러지도- even this; 못한다- can not

저러지도 못하네
Can't stand that either
저러지도- even that; V+네- (tag expressing surprise)

그저 바라보며 ba-ba-ba-baby
I just stare and say ba-ba-ba-baby
바라보다- to stare; V+며- and

매일 상상만 해 이름과 함께
Every day I only imagine without asking
매일- everyday; 상상- imagination; 함께- together

쓱 말을 났네 baby
I talk casually and say your name baby,
쓱- casually; 났네- place, release

아직 우린 모르는 사인데
But we don't even know each other
우린- we; 사인- relation

아무거나 걸쳐도 아름다워
Beautiful no matter what I wear
걸쳐- wear; 아름답다- to be beautiful

40

거울 속 단 둘이서 하는
Just the two of us in the mirror having a
거울- mirror; 속- in; 단- just
Fashion show show

이번엔 정말 꼭꼭 내가 먼저 talk talk
This time for sure, I'll be the first to talk talk
이번엔- This time; 정말- truly; 꼭꼭- surely; 먼저- first
다짐 뿐인걸 매번 다짐 뿐인걸
But it's only in my head, always only in my head
다짐- resolution; 뿐- only; 매번- many times

나나나나나나나 Nananananananana
콧노래가 나오다가 나도 몰래
I start humming and before I know it
콧노래- humming

눈물 날 것 같애
I feel like crying, I don't feel like myself
눈물- tears; 날- will come out
아닌 것 같애 내가 아닌 것 같애
This isn't like me at all, not at all
아닌- not; 것 같애- like
I love you so much

이미 난 다 컸다고 생각하는데
Think I'm all grown up now
이미- already; 컸다- grown
어쩌면 내 맘인데 왜
I'm free to make my own choices, but why
맘- mind; 어쩌면- somehow
내 맘대로 할 수 없는 건데
Why can't I have it my way
-대로- way
밀어내려고 하면 할수록
The more I try to push you away,
밀어내려고- push; ~면- if
자꾸 끌려 왜 자꾸 자꾸 끌려 baby
The more I'm drawn and attracted to you baby
자꾸- often; 끌려- attract, pull

I'm like TT, Just like TT
이런 내 맘 모르고 너무해
You don't know how I feel, So mean, so mean
너무해- do too much

I'm like TT, Just like TT
Tell me that you'll be my baby

어처구니 없다고 해
You say I'm ridiculous, (lit. Am I your girlfriend? You say you don't have a girlfriend.)
~니- (question tag); ~다고- say, tell
얼굴 값을 못한대
That I don't live up to my looks
얼굴- face; 값- price
전혀 위로 안돼 ba-ba-ba-baby
Doesn't cheer me up at all ba-ba-ba-baby
전혀- absolutely; 위로- cheer up

미칠 것 같애 이 와중에 왜
I'm going crazy in all this mess,
미칠- become crazy; 것- thing; 와중- midst
배는 또 고픈 건데
Why do I feel hungry?
배-stomach; 배고픈- hungry
하루 종일 먹기만 하는데
I eat all day and am still hungry
하루 종일- all day;먹다- to eat
맴매매매 아무 죄도 없는 Slap slap slap slap
죄- crime, offense
인형만 때찌
The innocent doll stings
인형- doll; 때찌다- to sting
종일 앉아있다가 엎드렸다
All day I sit like I'm fallen.
앉아있다가- as sit; V+다가- as...; 엎드렸다- felled

시간이 휙휙휙
Time flies flies flies
휙- (sound of passing air)

피부는 왜 이렇게 또 칙칙
What's with the dull skin again
피부- skin; 칙칙- dull

자꾸 틱틱 거리고 만 싶지
Keep wanting to just complain
자꾸- often; 틱틱- tic-i-tac

엄만 귀찮게 계속 왜왜왜왜왜
Mom keeps bothering me why why why?
엄만/엄마는- mother; 귀찮게- bothering

나나나나나나나 Nanananananana
콧노래가 나오다가 나도 몰래
I start humming and before I know it
콧노래- humming; 나오다- to come out

짜증날 것 같애 화날 것 같애
I feel so irritated, I'm so upset
짜증- frustration; 화- anger

이런 애가 아닌데
I'm normally not like this
애- kid

I love you so much

이미 난 다 컸다고 생각하는데
Think I'm all grown up now
컸다- grown

어쩌면 내 맘인데 왜
I'm free to make my own choices, but why

내 맘대로 할 수 없는 건데
Why can't I have it my way
밀어내려고 하면 할수록
The more I try to push you away,
자꾸 끌려 왜 자꾸 자꾸 끌려 baby
The more I'm drawn and attracted to you baby

I'm like TT, Just like TT

이런 내 맘 모르고 너무해 너무해
You don't know how I feel, so mean, so mean

I'm like TT, Just like TT

<u>Tell me that you'll be my baby</u>

혹시 이런 나를 알까요?
Do you realize what's going on inside me?
이런- this; 알까요- do you know?

이대로 사라져 버리면 안돼요
Don't disappear from my view like this
사라져- disappear; 안돼- not right

이번엔 정말 꼭꼭 내가 먼저 talk talk

이번엔- this time; 꼭꼭- well, without fail
This time for sure, I'll be the first to talk talk

다짐 뿐인걸 매번 다짐 뿐인걸
But it's only in my head, always only in my head
(lit. Only resolution, many times only resolution)
다짐- resolution

이미 난 다 컸다고 생각하는데
Think I'm all grown up now
어쩌면 내 맘인데 왜
Why can't I have it my way
내 맘대로 할 수 없는 건데
I'm free to make my own choices, but why
밀어내려고 하면 할수록
The more I try to push you away,
자꾸 끌려 왜 자꾸 자꾸 끌려 baby
The more I'm drawn and attracted to you baby

I'm like TT, Just like TT
이런 내 맘 모르고 너무해 너무해
<u>You don't know how I feel, so mean, so mean</u>
<u>I'm like TT, Just like TT</u>
<u>Tell me that you'll be my baby</u>

BTS- Fire

Jin, J-Hope, Jimin, Jungkook, Rap Monster, Suga, V

Lyrics/Translation/Notes

불타오르네
It's on fire!
불- fire; 타- burn; 오르네- start, occur

Fire, Fire, Fire, Fire

When I wake up in my room 난 뭣도 없지
When I wake up in my room, I have nothing
뭣도- whatever; ~지- of course (also commonly used as question tag)
해가 지고 난 후 비틀대며 걷지
After the sun sets, I sway as I walk
해- sun; 비틀다- to twist, sway; 걷다- step
다 만신창이로 취했어 취했어
I'm completely drunk, drunk
만신창- wreck; 취했어- drunk

막 욕해 길에서 길에서
I just swear from street to street
막- just; 욕해- swear; ~에서- at, on, from, to

나 맛이 갔지 미친놈 같지
I've lost it, I'm like a crazy guy
맛이- taste; 갔지- gone; 미친놈- crazy guy; 같지- like

다 엉망진창, livin' like 삐-이-
Everything's a mess, livin' like
다- all; 엉망진창- mess; 삐-이- (sound expressing a bit of mockery)
니 멋대로 살어 어차피 니 꺼야
Live however you want, it's yours anyway
니- yours; 멋- style, flavor; 대로- according to, as; 살다- live; 어차피- anyway
애쓰지 좀 말어 져도 괜찮아
Stop trying, it's okay to lose
애쓰지- try; 말어- stop; 져다- to lose; 괜찮아- okay

Errbody say La la la la la (La la la la la)
Say La la la la la (La la la la la)
손을 들어 소리칠러
Burn it up Throw your hands up, scream, burn it up
손- hand; 들다- to raise; 소리치다- to scream

불타오르네
It's on fire
불- fire; 타다- to burn

(Eh eh oh eh oh) (Eh eh oh eh oh)

싹 다 불태워라 Bow wow wow
Set everything on fire, bow wow wow
싹- completely
(Eh eh oh eh oh) (Eh eh oh eh oh)
싹 다 불태워라 Bow wow wow
Set everything on fire, bow wow wow

Hey, burn it up 전부 다 태울 것 같이
Hey, burn it up Like you're gonna set everything on fire
전부- all, everything; 태우다- to burn (~울 is future tag)
Hey, turn it up 새벽이 다 갈 때까지
Hey, turn it up Until the dawn is gone
새벽- dawn; ~까지- to, until; 갈 때- when (it will) be gone

그냥 살아도 돼 우린 젊기에
Just live because we're young

그냥- just; 돼- okay; 젊기에- because young

그 말하는 넌 뭔 수저길래
Who are you to compare me with others?

수저- spoon and chopsticks (lingo used to describe objectifying a person as in "What am I to you? Just spoon and chopsticks?")

수저수저 거려 난 사람인데
Used as a thing, I'm a human.

사람- person

(So what~)

니 멋대로 살어 어차피 니 꺼야
Live however you want, it's yours anyway

애쓰지 좀 말어 져도 괜찮아
Stop trying, it's okay to lose

Errbody say La la la la la (La la la la la)
Say La la la la la (La la la la la)
손을 들어 소리질러
Burn it up Throw your hands up, scream, burn it up

불타오르네 It's on fire

(Eh eh oh eh oh)
싹 다 불태워라 Bow wow wow
Set everything on fire, bow wow wow

(Eh eh oh eh oh)
싹 다 불태워라 Bow wow wow
Set everything on fire, bow wow wow

(Fire) 겁 많은 자여 여기로(Fire)
All you with a lot of fear, come here

겁- fear; 여기- here

 (Fire) 괴로운 자여 여기로(Fire)
All you who are suffering, come here

괴로운- suffering

(Fire) 맨주먹을 들고
All night long (Fire) Lift up your fists, all night long

맨- last; 주먹- fist

(Fire) 진군하는 발걸음으로
(Fire) With marching footsteps

발걸음- step; ~으로- through, by, with

(Fire) 뛰어봐 미쳐버려 다
(Fire) Run and go crazy
뛰어- jump, run; ~봐- try, see

싹 다 불태워라 Bow wow wow
Set everything on fire, bow wow wow
싹 다 불태워라 Bow wow wow
Set everything on fire, bow wow wow

(Fire Fire)
싹 다 불태워라 Bow wow wow
Set everything on fire, bow wow wow
(Fire Fire)
싹 다 불태워라 Bow wow wow
Set everything on fire, bow wow wow
(Fire Fire)
싹 다 불태워라 Bow wow wow
Set everything on fire, bow wow wow

용서해줄게
I'll forgive you

싹 다 불태워라 Bow wow wow
Set everything on fire, bow wow wow

BTS- Danger

Lyrics/Translation/Notes

You in danger
You in danger
You in danger
You in danger

맨날 이런 식
You're always like this
맨날- always; 이런- this; 식- condition, order

너는 너 나는 나 너의 공식
You are you, I am me, your formula
N+의- (possessive tag); 공식- formula

핸드폰은 장식
My phone is just a mere accessory
장식- decoration, accessory

나 남친이 맞긴 하니? I'm sick
I'm sick Am I really your boyfriend? I'm sick
남친- boyfriend; V+니- (question tag)

왜 숙제처럼 표현들을 미뤄
Why do you push off expressing your feelings like homework?

숙제- homework; N+처럼- like; 표현-expression; 미뤄- postpone

우리 무슨 Business? 아님 내가 싫어?

Are we in a business relationship? Or do you not like me?

무슨- which, what; 아님- if not, or; 싫어- don't like

덩 덩 디기 덩 덩

(Sound made when Korean drums are beaten)

좀 살가워져라 오늘도 또 주문을 빌어

Please be kinder, I'll request it again today

살갑다- to be affectionate; 오늘- today; 주문- order; 빌다- to beg

우린 평행선

We are parallel lines

평행선- parallel lines

같은 곳을 보지만 넌 다르지

We look at the same place but are so different

같은- alike; 곳- place; 보(지만)- look(but); 다르다- to be different

난 너밖에 없는데

I don't have anyone but you

밖에- outside of

왜 너 밖에 있는 것만 같은지

But why does it feel like I'm outside of you?

~지- (question form ending)

꽁하면 넌 물어 "삐쳤니?"

If I stay quiet, you ask, "Are you mad?"

물어- ask; 삐쳤니- are you mad(sulking)?

날 삐치게 했던 적이나 있었니?

Well, did you even pretend to make me mad?

적하다- to pretend

넌 귀요미 난 지못미

You're a cutie and I am pitiful

귀요미- cutie; 지못미- pitiful person

생기길 니가 더 사랑하는 기적이

I hope for a miracle of you loving me more than I love you

생기길 – creative path; 사랑-love; 기적- miracle

넌 내가 없는데 난 너로 가득해

You don't have me but I'm filled with you

없는데- lacking, without

미칠 것 같아 Whoa
whoa It's driving me crazy
미치다- to go mad, crazy

근데 왜 이러는데 왜 바보 만들어
Then, why are you doing this? Why are you making me into a fool?
근데- then; 이러는데- this; 바보- a fool; 만들다- to make

나 이제 경고해 헷갈리게 하지 마
I'm warning you now, stop confusing me
이제- now; 경고해- warn; 헷갈리게- confuse; 하지 마- don't

장난해 너? 도대체 내가 뭐야?
Are you joking? What am I to you?
장난해- fool, toy with; 도대체- indeed

만만해 Uh? 날 갖고 노는 거야?
Am I easy to you? Are you playing with me?
만만해 – trifle with; 갖고- take; 노는- playful; 거야- thing

너 지금 위험해 왜 나를 시험해?
You're in danger right now, why are you testing me?
위험해- endanger; 시험해- test

왜 나를 시험해? 헷갈리게 하지 마
Why are you testing me? Stop confusing me

장난해 너? 도대체 내가 뭐야?
Are you joking? What am I to you?
만만해 Uh? 날 갖고 노는 거야?
Am I easy to you? Are you playing with me?
너 지금 위험해 왜 나를 시험해?
You're in danger right now, why are you testing me?
왜 나를 시험해? 헷갈리게 하지 마
Why are you testing me? Stop confusing me

너 땜에 너무 아파
It hurts so much because of you
땜에- because of; 아파- hurt

너 땜에 너무 아파
It hurts so much because of you
너 땜에 너무 아파
It hurts so much because of you

헷갈리게 하지 마
Stop confusing me
헷갈리다- to confuse; 하지 마- don't do

너 내게 너무 나빠
You're so bad to me
너- you; 내게- to me; 너무- so, too; 나빠- bad

너 내게 너무 나빠
You're so bad to me

너 내게 너무 나빠
You're so bad to me

헷갈리게 하지 마
Stop confusing me

연락 부재중 Unlock 수배 중
You're not answering, I'm looking for how to unlock you
부재중- absence; 수배 중- wanting

너란 여자 본심을 수색 중
I'm investigating a girl like you and your true feelings
~란/랑- with; 여자- girl; 본심- true feeling; 수색 – investigation; 중- during

고작 보내 준 게 문자 두세 줄
All you send me is a line or two through text
고작- only; 보내- send; 준- given; 게- it, thing; 문자- text, letter; 두- two; 세- three

이게 내가 바랬던 연애 꿈?
Is this the relationship and dream that I've wanted?
바랬던- hoped for; 연애- relationship; 꿈- dream

파란만장 Love story 다 어디 갔나?
Where did my exciting love story go?
파란만장- blue ups and downs(thrilling)

Drama 에 나온 주인공들 다 저리 가라
Move out of the way, drama characters
주인공- actors, characters; 들- (plural tag); 저리- there

너 때문에 수백 번 쥐어 잡는 머리카락
I rip out my hair hundreds of times because of you
수백- hundreds; 번- times; 쥐어 잡는- grab and pull out; 머리카락- hair

너 담담 그저 당당 날 차 빵빵
But you don't care, you think it's fine and you kick me (lit. You're calm, just confident, me a car pang, pang)
담담- calm; 그저- just; 당당- confident; 차- car

뭐니 뭐니 난 네게 뭐니?
What, what, what am I to you?
뭐니- what?

너보다 니 친구에게 전해 듣는 소식
I hear about you from your friends rather than you
-보다- than; 전해- transmit; 소식- news

원해 원해 Huh 너를 원해
I want you, I want you, huh, I want you
원해- want

너란 여잔 사기꾼 내 맘을 흔든 범인
A girl like you, a con-artist, a criminal who shook my heart
사기꾼- con artist, fraud; 흔든- shaken; 범인- criminal

불이 붙기 전부터 내 맘 다 쓰고
You used up my heart before the fire even started
전- before; -부터- from; 쓰다- to use

일방적인 구애들 해 봤자 헛수고
I can try to have a one-sided relationship but it'll be useless
일방적인- one sided; 구애들- lovers; 해 봤자- try; 헛수고- useless

너에게 난 그저 연인이 아닌 우정이 편했을지도 몰라 I'm a love loser
Maybe you're more comfortable with being friends instead of lovers, I'm a love loser
연인- lovers; 아닌- not; 우정- friendship; 편하다- to be comfortable

넌 내가 없는데 난 너로 가득해
You don't have me but I'm filled with you
미칠 것 같아 Whoa whoa
It's driving me crazy Whoa whoa
근데 왜 이러는데 왜 바보 만들어
Why are you doing this? Why are you making me into a fool?

나 이제 경고해 헷갈리게 하지 마
I'm warning you now, stop confusing me
장난해 너? 도대체 내가 뭐야?
Are you joking? What am I to you?
만만해 Uh? 날 갖고 노는 거야?
Am I easy to you? Are you playing with me?
너 지금 위험해 왜 나를 시험해?
You're in danger right now, why are you testing me?
왜 나를 시험해? 헷갈리게 하지 마
Why are you testing me? Stop confusing me

장난해 너? 도대체 내가 뭐야?
Are you joking? What am I to you?
만만해 Uh? 날 갖고 노는 거야?
Am I easy to you? Are you playing with me?

너 지금 위험해 왜 나를 시험해?
You're in danger right now, why are you testing me?
왜 나를 시험해? 헷갈리게 하지 마
Why are you testing me? Stop confusing me

너 땜에 너무 아파
It hurts so much because of you
너 땜에 너무 아파
It hurts so much because of you
너 땜에 너무 아파
It hurts so much because of you

헷갈리게 하지 마
Stop confusing me
너 내게 너무 나빠
You're so bad to me
너 내게 너무 나빠
You're so bad to me
너 내게 너무 나빠
You're so bad to me
헷갈리게 하지 마
Stop confusing me

Black Pink- Playing with Fire

Rose, Jennie, Jisoo, Lisa

Lyrics/Translation/Notes

우리 엄만 매일 내게 말했어
My mom told me every day
우리- our; 엄만- mom; 매일- every day

언제나 남자 조심하라고
To always be careful of guys
언제나- whenever; 남자- man; 조심하다- be careful

사랑은 마치 불장난 같아서
Because love is like playing with fire
사랑- long; 마치- as if; 불- fire; 장난- toy, play 같아서- is like

다치니까
I'll get hurt
다치다- to get hurt; V+니까- because...

엄마 말이 꼭 맞을지도 몰라
My mom might be right
말- talk, words; V+ㄹ/을지도 몰라- don't know...

널 보면 내 맘이 뜨겁게 달아올라
Because when I see you, my heart gets hot
보다- to see; 뜨겁게- hot

두려움보단 널 향한 끌림이 더 크니까
Because rather than fear my attraction to you is bigger

두려움- fear; 보단(보다는)- than; 향한- toward; 끌림- attraction; 큰- big

멈출 수 없는 이 떨림은
I can't stop this trembling
멈추다- to stop; 떨림- trembling
On and on and on
내 전부를 너란 세상에
I, into your world,
전부- all; 세상- world
다 던지고 싶어
wanna throw my all
던지다- to throw; V+고 싶어- want…

Look at me look at me now
이렇게 넌 날 애태우고 있잖아
You are burning me up like this
애태우다- to feel nervous; V+잖아- (tag meaning "as you know…", "you should know…")
끌 수 없어
I can't turn it off
끄다- to switch off
우리 사랑은 불장난
Our love that's like playing with fire

My love is on fire

Now burn baby burn
불장난
Playing with fire

My love is on fire
So, don't play with me boy
불장난
Playing with fire
장난- game

Oh no 난 이미 멀리 와버렸는걸
Oh no, I've already come too far
이미- already; 멀리- far
어느새 이 모든 게 장난이 아닌 걸
Suddenly, none of this is a game anymore
어느새 – before I know, suddenly; 이- this

사랑이란 빨간 불씨
Love is like red fire
빨간- red, 씨- seed, lineage

불어라 바람 더 커져가는 불길
Blow, wind, so the flames will grow
불어라 – blow; 바람- wind; 불길- flames

이게 약인지 독인지 우리 엄마도 몰라
Is this medicine or poison? Not even my mom knows
약- medicine; ~인지...~인지- or; 독- poison; 몰라- don't know

내 맘 도둑인데 왜 경찰도 몰라
A robber in my heart, why don't the police know?
도둑- thief; 인데- is; 경찰- police

불 붙은 내 심장에 더 부어라 너란 기름
Pour out your oil in my burning heart
심장- fire; 붓다- to pour; 기름- oil
Kiss him will I diss him
I don't know but I miss him
중독을 넘어선 이 사랑은 crack
This is past addiction, this love is crack
중독- addiction; 넘어선- gotten past
내 심장의 색깔은 black
The color of my heart is black
색깔- color

멈출 수 없는 이 떨림은
I can't stop this trembling
On and on and on
내 전부를 너란 불길 속으로
I, all, into your flames

던지고 싶어
want to throw.

Look at me look at me now
이렇게 넌 날 애태우고 있잖아
You are burning me up like this
~잖아- don't you know
끌 수 없어
I can't turn it off

우리 사랑은 불장난
Our love that's like playing with fire

My love is on fire
Now burn baby burn
불장난
Playing with fire
My love is on fire
So, don't play with me boy
불장난
Playing with fire

걷잡을 수가 없는 걸
I can't control it
걷잡다- to handle, grab

너무나 빨리 퍼져 가는 이 불길
This fire path is spreading too quickly
퍼져- spreading

이런 날 멈추지 마
Don't stop me
마- don't

이 사랑이 오늘 밤을 태워버리게
Woo So this love can burn up this night
밤- night; 태워버리다- to burn up

Black Pink- Stay

Lyrics/Translation/Notes

툭하면 거친 말들로
So easily, with harsh words
툭하다- to provoke; 거친- harsh

내 맘에 상처를 내놓고
You put scars in my heart
상처- injury; 내놓다- to put down

미안하단 말 한마디 없이
Without even saying sorry
미안하다- to say sorry; 한마디- one word; 없이- without

또 나 혼자 위로하고
Again, I'm comforting myself
혼자- alone; 위로하다- to comfort

오늘 하루도 혹시 날 떠날까 늘 불안해 해
All day, always nervous you're going to leave me
오늘- today; 하루- all day; 혹시- by any chance; 떠나다- to leave

늘- always; 불안하다- to be nervous

I just want you to stay
점점 무뎌져 가는
That's getting more and more dull
점점- little by little; 무뎌져- dull

너의 그 무표정 속에
In your expressionless face
무- none; 표정- facial expression

천천히 내려놓자며
Let's slowly let this go
천천히- slowly; 내리다- to lower; 놓다- to place

거울에 속삭이곤 해
I whisper to the mirror,
거울- mirror; 속삭하다- to whisper

날 당연하게 생각하는 너지만
You take me for granted
당연하게- granted

그게 너다워 그래도
But that's you, but still
다워- warm

Stay stay stay with me

널 닮은 듯한 슬픈 멜로디
This sad melody resembles you
닮은- resembling; 듯- meaning; 슬픈- sad; 멜로디- melody

이렇게 날 울리는데 eh eh
It makes me cry eh eh
울리는- crying

네 향기는 달콤한 felony
Your scent is a sweet felony
향기- scent; 달콤한- sweet

너무 밉지만 사랑해
I hate you so much but i love you
밉다- to hate

어두운 밤이 날 가두기 전에
Before the dark night traps me in
어두운- dark; 가두기- confinement

내 곁을 떠나지마
Don't leave my side
곁- side; 떠나지마- don't leave

아직 날 사랑하니 내 맘과 같다면
Do you still love me? If you feel the same
아직- still

오늘은 떠나지마
Don't leave today

굳이 너여야만 하는 이유는 묻지마
Don't ask why it has to be you
굳이- if you ask; 여야- should; 이유- should; 묻다- to ask

그저 내 곁에 stay with me
Just stay with me

(It goes a little something like)
Lalalalalala Lalalalalala Lalalalalala
Lalalalalala Lalalalalala Lalalalalala

지금 당장 많은 걸 바라는 게 아냐
I don't expect a lot right now
당장- just no; 바라는- hoping

그저 내 곁에 stay with me
Just stay with me

사실은 난 더 바라는 게 없어 이제
There's nothing more I want now
사실은- in fact, 바라는 게- thing that is wanted

심장은 뛰긴 하는 건지 무감각해 그래
I can't even tell if my heart is beating
뛰긴- beating; 무감각해- can't feel

사람들과의 억지스런 한마디보단
Rather than forceful conversations with others
-과- with; 억지스런- forced; 보단(보다)- than

너와의 어색한 침묵이 차라리 좋아
I'd rather be in awkward silence with you
어색한- awkward; 침묵- silence; 차라리- rather

So, stay 그게 어디가 됐건 말이야
So, stay, wherever that may be
어디가- wherever; 됐건- became

가끔 어둠이 올 때면 I'll be your fire
Sometimes, when darkness comes, I'll be your fire
가끔- sometimes; 때- when

거짓 같은 세상 속 유일한 truth it's you
In this world that is a lie the only truth, it's you
거짓- lie; 유일한- only
This a letter from me to you

널 닮은 듯한 슬픈 멜로디
This sad melody resembles you
이렇게 날 울리는데 eh eh
It makes me cry eh eh
네 향기는 달콤한 felony
Your scent is a sweet felony
너무 밉지만 사랑해
I hate you so much but i love you

어두운 밤이 날 가두기 전에
Before the dark night traps me in
내 곁을 떠나지마
Don't leave me
아직 날 사랑하니 내 맘과 같다면
Do you still love me? If you feel the same
오늘은 떠나지마
Don't leave today

굳이 너여야만 하는 이유는 묻지마
Don't ask why it has to be you
그저 내 곁에 stay with me
Just stay with me
(It goes a little something like)
Lalalalalala Lalalalalala Lalalalalala
Lalalalalala Lalalalalala Lalalalalala

지금 당장 많은걸 바라는 게 아냐
I don't expect a lot right now
그저 내 곁에 stay with me
Just stay with me

(It goes a little something like)
Lalalalalala Lalalalalala Lalalalalala
Lalalalalala Lalalalalala Lalalalalala

지금 당장 많은걸 바라는 게 아냐
I don't expect a lot right now

그저 내 곁에 stay with me
Just stay with me

NCT U- The 7th Sense

Ten, Do Young, Mark, Haechan, Taeil, Taeyong, Yuta

Lyrics/Translation/Notes

차가운 세상 두 눈을 감고
In this cold world, I'm closing my eyes
차가운- cold; 세상- world; 눈- eye; 감다- to close

침대에 누워 두 귀를 막고
Laying down in bed, covering my ears
침대- bed; 누워- lay; 귀- ear; 막다- to block

어제가 오늘 또 오늘이 어제
Yesterday is today, today is yesterday
어제- yesterday

때늦은 자책만 가득한 채
I'm only filled with late self-guilt
때늦은- late; 자책- self-guilt; 채- state of, situation

We'll take it slow
Baby, baby we'll take it slow
Oh

같은 꿈 마치 날 부르는
In the same dream, I hear a familiar
꿈- dream; 마치- as if; 부르는- full

익숙한 노래 마침내 연결돼
song that calls to me, it connects us
익숙한- familiar, used to; 노래- song; 마침내- finally; 연결돼- connected

감싸주지 나를
Hate is on me It wraps around me, hate is on me
감싸주지- give appreciation
반복되는 매일도 괜찮다고
Each day repeats but it's okay
반복되는- became repeated; 괜찮다- to be okay
깊은 어둠 위를 걸어
I'm walking on top of a deep darkness
깊은- deep; 위- above, up
저 너머에 숨겨진 진짜를 봐
Look at what is real, that's hidden over there
너머에- over there; 숨겨진- hidden; 진짜- truth

Open your eyes 조용히 Open your eyes
Open your eyes, quietly open your eyes

(조용히 Open your eyes)

Open your eyes 이제는 Open your eyes
Open your eyes, now open your eyes

(이제는 Open your eyes)

Open your eyes 조용히 Open your eyes
Open your eyes, quietly open your eyes

(조용히 Open your eyes)

Open your eyes 이제는 Open your eyes
Open your eyes, now open your eyes

Yeah, yeah~

버려지지 않는 미움과 나를 괴롭히는 꿈
Hatred that will not go away and dreams that torture me
괴롭히는- tortured; 꿈- dream
저 시계는 나를 비웃듯 한 치 오차 없이 가
The clock laughs at me, it does not give a single error

시계- clock; 비웃다- to laugh at, scold; 치- trembling; 오차- error

<u>(Oh yeah)</u>
엉망진창 나도 날 모르겠어
I'm a mess, I don't even know myself,
엉망진창- mess; ~겠어- would, will

어둡게 색칠 된 미래
my future is colored darkly
어둡게- darkly; 미래- future

허우적대 더 새까맣게 이 밤에 덧칠을 해
I'm struggling, coloring this night even blacker,
허우적대- struggling; 새까맣게- black; 덧칠하다- to cover, paint over

<u>Ooh yeah</u>

차가운 세상 두 눈을 감고
In this cold world, I'm closing my eyes
침대에 누워 두 귀를 막고
Laying down in bed, covering my ears
어제가 오늘 또 오늘이 어제
Yesterday is today, today is yesterday
때늦은 자책만 가득한 채
I'm only filled with late self-guilt

We'll take it slow
(We'll take it slow, take it slow)
Baby, baby we'll take it slow
Oh~
같은 꿈 마치 날 부르는
In the same dream, I hear a familiar
익숙한 노래 (You do)
song that calls to me (You do)
마침내 연결돼 (You want)
It connects us

Uh 여전히 어딘가로
Uh, I'm still somewhere (You want)
여전히- forever

이름 모를 지역에 난 이름 모를 Hall 로
To an unknown place, to an unknown hall
이름- name; 지역에- area, place

몇 밤을 자도 편치 않은 어딘가 에서도
After several nights, in a place that's uncomfortable
몇- several, some; 편치 않은- uncongenial, discomforting

결국 대부분 내 시간을 보내는 Explorer
I'm spending most of my time, explorer.
결국- finally, in conclusion; 대부분- usually; 보내는- sending

Uh, and that's a long ass ride

정신없이 휘둘리다 결국 눈을 감지
Mindlessly going around until I close my eyes
정신(없이)- mind(without); 휘둘리다- to go around

꿈과 지금 사이를 또 한번 의심하고
I'm doubting this moment, between dreams and reality
사이- between; 한번- one time; 의심하고- doubting

난 또 확인할 게 있어 바로
I have something else to check,
확인- check, confirmation; 바로- immediately

지금 너와 같이, Uh
just like you right now, uh

Open your eyes 조용히 Open your eyes
Open your eyes, quietly open your eyes
(조용히 Open your eyes) (Quietly open your eyes)

Open your eyes 이제는 Open your eyes
Open your eyes, quietly open your eyes

(Open your eyes) Open your eyes, now open your eyes
Open your eyes, now open your eyes

Open your eyes 조용히 Open your eyes

(조용히 Open your eyes)

Open your eyes 이제는 Open your eyes

난해한 저 불규칙 속에 (속에)
Inside the irregularity that's hard to understand (Inside)
불규칙- irregular

깊이 가려져왔던 (가려진)
Story There's a story that's deeply hidden (Hidden)
깊이- deep; 가려져왔던- be covered

눈을 뜨네 이 노랠 통해
Eyes are being opened through this song

뜨네- opened; 통해- through

읽혀 지는 너의 꿈 (꿈)
Your dreams are being read (Dreams)
읽다- to read

긴 잠에서 깨어난 (난)
I've been awakened from a deep sleep (Awakened)
긴-long; 잠- sleep; 깨어난- awakened

내 일곱 번째의 감각
My seventh sense
일곱- seven; 번째- time (count); ~의- (possessive marker); 감각- sense

Oh 내 곁에 다가와 펼쳐진 밤
Oh, this night came to my side
곁에- side; 다가와- come closer; 펼쳐진- spread

조금씩 가까워 지는 다른 꿈
Little by little, a different dream is getting closer
조금씩- little by little; 가까워- closer; 다른- different

이해가 돼 모두가 내 것처럼 다
Now I understand, as if everything is mine
내 것처럼- as if mine; 이해- understanding

Open your eyes
진짜를 봐 Open your eyes
Look at what's real, open your eyes

Open your eyes
Open your eyes (혼자가 아니야 난 I, I)
Open your eyes (I'm not alone I, I)

Got7- Just Right

JB, Jinyoung, Taeil, Yugyeom, Bam Bam, Mark

Lyrics/Translation/Notes

Baby, you are just...
Just right
거울아 거울아 제발 좀 말해주려무나
Mirror, mirror please tell her
제발- please

저울아 너도 말해주려무나
Scale, please tell her too
저울- scale

아무것도 바꿀 필요 없이 예쁘다고
That she doesn't need to change anything
아무것- anything; 바꿀- change; 필요하다- to need; 예쁘다- to be pretty

지금 그 모습 그대로 완벽하다고
That she's pretty and perfect just as she is right now
모습- appearance; 완벽하다- to be perfect

마냥 행복하면 돼 걱정 없이
Just be happy, don't worry
마냥- just; 행복- happiness; 걱정- worry

부족한 점이 뭔지 찾기 없기
Whatever the flaws; without searching
부족- lack; 점- point, spot; 찾다- to find

거울 대신 그냥 내 눈 빛을 바라봐
Instead of the mirror, just look into my eyes
대신- instead; 그냥- just

저울 대신 내 등 위에 올라타봐 봐
Instead of the scale, just get on my back
등- back; 위에- for; 올라타- get on

아무리 널 뜯어봐도
No matter how much you're taken apart
아무리- no matter; 뜯어하다- to tear

보고 또 보고 또 봐도
Looking and again looking
보다- to look; -고- and

니가 말하는 안 예쁜 부분이 어딘지
Where is the person who calls you unpretty?
부분- person

그게 어딘지 찾을 수가 없어 난
I can't find that part of you
그게- that; 찾을 수가 없어- can't find

지금처럼 만만만만만 만
Like now just just just
만- only, just

있어주면 난난난난난
You remain, you you you
있어- is, are

바랄게 없으니 넌 아무것도
Since I want nothing, anything about you
바랄게- something wanted; 게- thing

바꾸지 마마마마마
don't change, don't don't don't
바꾸지- change; 마- don't

아무 걱정마마마마마마
Don't worry about anything, don't don't don't
너의 모든게 다다다다
Your everything all, all, all

너의- your

다 좋으니까 너는 아무것도 바꾸지 마마마마마
all good, so don't change anything about yourself, don't don't don't

이대로 (지금 이대로) 오 (그냥 이대로)
Just as you are (right now) oh (just as you are)
이대로- like this

오 (지금 이대로) 오오오 있으면 돼
Oh (just as you are right now) just stay as you are
있으면- if it is; 돼- right, proper

딱 좋아 너의 모든 게 그러니 네 맘
Everything about you is just right
딱- just

놓아 아무 걱정하지 마 이 말
So relax, stop worrying, these words
놓아- relax, put down

백 퍼센트 다 그대로 믿어도 돼
good to believe as it is 100%
백- 100; 퍼센트- percent; 믿다- to believe

모든 걱정 백 퍼센트 다 지워도 돼
Fine to erase all of your worries 100%
지워하다- to delete, erase

아무리 널 뜯어봐도
No matter how much you're taken apart
보고 또 보고 또 봐도
Looking and again looking
니가 말하는 안 예쁜 부분이 어딘지
Where is the person who calls you unpretty?
그게 어딘지 찾을 수가 없어 난
I can't find that part of you

지금처럼 만만만만만 만
Like now just, just, just
있어주면 난난난난난
You remain, you, you, you
바랄게 없으니 넌 아무것도
Since I want nothing, anything about you
바꾸지 마마마마마
don't change, don't don't don't

아무 걱정마마마마마마
Don't worry about anything, don't don't don't
너의 모든게 다다다다
Your everything all, all, all
다 좋으니까 너는 아무것도
I like all; you anything
바꾸지 마마마마마마 about yourself
don't change, don't don't don't

이대로 (지금 이대로) 오 (그냥 이대로)
Just as you are (right now) oh (just as you are)
오 (지금 이대로) 오오오 있으면 돼
Oh (just as you are right now) just stay as you are

옥에 티도 티가 나야 찾는 거지 원
I'd find a flaw if there was even a flaw that I could see
옥에 티도- (Korean expression meaning "a fly in the ointment")
눈부시게 빛나 빈틈이 없지 넌
You dazzle, you have nothing missing
눈부시게 빛나- dazzle; 빈틈이- emptiness
내 눈에 얼마나 예쁜지 I want you
Do you know how pretty you are in my eyes? I want you
눈- eye; 얼마나- how much
지금 이대로 you're the only one
Just as you are, you're the only one

옥에 티도 티가 나야 찾는 거지 원
I'd find a flaw if there was even a flaw that I could see
눈부시게 빛나 빈틈이 없지 넌
You dazzle, you have nothing missing
내 눈에 얼마나 예쁜지 I want you
I want you Do you know how pretty you are in my eyes? I want you
지금 이대로 you're the only one
Just as you are, you're the only one

지금처럼 만만만만만 만
Like now just, just, just
있어주면 난난난난난
You remain, you, you, you
바랄게 없으니 넌 아무것도
Since I want nothing, anything about you

72

바꾸지 마마마마마
don't change, don't don't don't
아무 걱정마마마마마마
Don't worry about anything, don't don't don't
너의 모든게 다다다다
Your everything all, all, all
다 좋으니까 너는 아무것도
I like all; you anything
바꾸지 마마마마마 about yourself
don't change, don't don't don't

Red Velvet- Russian Roulette

Joy, Irene, Seulgi, Yeri, Wendy

Lyrics/Translation/Notes

La La La La La La La La La La La La La
La La La La La La La La La La La La La
날카로운 Secret 둘러싼 얘긴
Surrounded by a sharp secret
날카로운- sharp; 둘러싼- surrounded

베일 속에
Behind a veil
베일- veil

점점 더 깊은 H H Hush 맘을 겨눠이제 Aiming for your heart now
Deeper and deeper, h-h-hush
깊은- deep; 겨눠- aim

여긴 온통 어두운 밤 하늘색
This place is the color of a dark night
여긴- here; 온통- everywhere; 어두운- dark; 밤- night; 하늘색- sky color
그림자조차 길을 잃게 해
Even the shadows get lost
그림자- shadow; ~조차- even (often used to unexpected occurences)

Oh 넌 항상 Love is game 쉽게 즐기는 가벼움일 뿐이라고
You say it's light and easily enjoyed
쉽게- easily; 즐기는- enjoyable; 가벼움- light; 일- work; 뿐- only; -라고- say

뭐 이렇게 못된 얘기로 자꾸
Why do you keep saying these bad things
뭐- what; 이렇게- like this; 못된- wretched, bad; 얘기- talk, words; 자꾸- often

피해 가려고만 하니 왜
Trying to avoid me?
자꾸- often; 피해- avoid; 가려고만- only go

커지는 Heart B B Beat
Growing heart b-b-beat

빨라지는데
It's getting faster

너답지 않게 Heart B B B Beat Not like you, heart b-b-b-beat 거려
답지- answer

나를 볼 때
Whenever you see me

마지막 남은 순간까지
Till the very last moment
마지막- final; 남은- remaining; 순간- moment

점점 다가오지
Crazy It comes closer and closer, crazy
다가오지- closer

아찔하게 겨눈 러시안 룰렛
The risky aim, Russian Roulette
아찔하게- giddy; 겨눈- aim

Ah Ah Ah Yeah
La La La La La La La La La La La La
나 이미 Heart B B B Beat
이미- already

마지막 남은 순간까지
Until the very last moment
내게 맡기게 될 거야 넌
You'll have to trust me
맡기게- trust; 될- become
달콤한 너의 러시안 룰렛

I'm your sweet Russian Roulette
달콤한- sweet

반짝인 Secret
A dazzling secret
더 이상 외면하진 못 해
You can't turn away from it anymore
이상- anymore; 외면하다- to turn away

버튼은 내가 P P Push 받아들여이제
I'll p-p-push your button; accept it now
받아들여- accept

네 맘 온통 내 모습 채워지게
So your heart can be filled with me
모습- appearance; 채워지게- filled
꿈 꿀 때조차 나를 찾게 돼
You'll look for me even when you're dreaming
꿈- dream; 꿀- dreaming; 때- time; -조차- as, in the process of; 찾다- to find

Oh 아직 넌 Love is game
Oh you still say, love is game
아직- still
내게 말해도 흔들려 네 목소리도
You tell me but your voice is shaking
흔들려- shake, confuse; 목소리- voice

장난스레 스친 눈빛 너머로
Past the playful eyes
장난스레- playful; 스친- grazed, flashed; 눈빛- eyelight
어쩔 줄 모르는 네 모습
I see you, not knowing what to do
어쩔- what; 줄- way; 모르는- not knowing

커지는 Heart B B Beat
Growing heart b-b-beat
빨라지는데
It's getting faster
너답지 않게 Heart B B B Beat 거려
Not like you, heart b-b-b-beat
나를 볼 때
Whenever you see me

마지막 남은 순간까지
Till the very last moment
점점 다가오지 Crazy
It comes closer and closer, crazy
아찔하게 겨눈 러시안 룰렛
The risky aim, Russian Roulette

Ah Ah Ah Yeah
La La La La La La La La La La La La La
나 이미 Heart B B B Beat

마지막 남은 순간까지
Until the very last moment
내게 맡기게 될 거야 넌
You'll have to trust me
달콤한 너의 러시안 룰렛
I'm your sweet Russian Roulette

이토록 깊은 꿈이 넌 처음일 걸
You never had this deep of a dream before
이토록- this; 처음- first
내 맘이 이 밤이 아른거리는
Game My heart and this night makes this game flicker
아른거리다- to flicker, to waver
You can't control

커지는 Heart B B Beat
Growing heart b-b-beat
빨라지는데
It's getting faster
터질듯한 Heart B B B Beat
About to explode Heart B-B-B-Beat
터지다- to explode; 터질듯한- as if to explode
Key 는 내가 쥘게
I'll hold onto the key

마지막 남은 순간까지
Till the very last moment
점점 다가오지 Crazy
It comes closer and closer, crazy
아찔하게 겨눈 러시안 룰렛
The risky aim, Russian Roulette

Ah Ah Ah Yeah
La La La La La La La La La La La La La

나이미 Heart B B B Beat
마침내 빼낼 수도 없게 박혀
It's already engraved in you, can't take it out
네 심장 더 깊은 곳
Deeper in your heart
달콤한 너의 러시안 룰렛
I'm your sweet Russian Roulette

커지는 Heart B B Beat
Growing heart b-b-beat
빨라지는데
It's getting faster

La La La La La La La La La La La La La
커지는 Heart B B Beat
Growing heart b-b-beat

빨라지는데
It's getting faster

La La La La La
Heart B B B Beat

Infinite- The Eye

Dongwoo, Hoya, L, Woohyun, Sungyeol, Sungjong, Sungkyu

Lyrics/Translation/Notes

Okay, okay

다 끝났다 다 잊었다
It's all over, I forgot it all
끝났다- finished; 잊었다- forgot

이제야 너를 지운다
Finally, I've erased you
지운다- erased

참 길었던 참 힘들었던
It was so long, it was so hard
참- so; 길(었던)- long(I remember); 힘들다- to be difficult; ~던/었던- (past adjective marker suggesting recall or memory of what's described)

이별과 이별한다
Goodbye to goodbye
이별- separation; -과- with

다 그쳤다 다 멎었다
It has all ended, it has all stopped
그쳤다- ended; 멎었다- stopped

79

이제야 빛이 내린다
Finally, light is coming down
빛- light; 내린다- coming down

태풍 같던 비바람이
The storm like rain and wind
태풍- typhoon; 비- rain; 바람- wind

이제야 끝났는데
Has finally stopped but

너의 기억이 추억이
Your remembrences, memories
기억이- remembrance; 추억- memory

다시 나를 휘감아
Wrap around me again
다시- again; 휘감아- wrap around

한발만 가도 난
Even when I take one step
한발- step; ~만- only

온통 너로 또 젖잖아
I get drenched with you
젖잖아- drenched; ~로- by, with

네게서 떠나온 곳이
The place I left you
~게서- from; 떠나온- left; 곳이- place

도망쳐 달려온 곳이
The place I ran away from
도망쳐- escaped; 달려온- ran and come

너의 기억 속 중심이란 걸
It's the center of my memories of you
중심- center

이제 깨닫는다
I finally realize
깨닫다- to realize

끝내지 못한 이별 뒤
After a break up that hasn't ended
끝내지- end; 못한- can't; 뒤- after

이별과 이별
Goodbye with goodbye

내게 남겨진 인연과 인연
The fate with fate that lasts with me
남겨진- remained; 인연과- fate

너를 벗어나려 해도
Even when I try to escape from you
멀리 도망치려 해도
Even when I try to run far away
멀리- far away

또 휩쓸려 네게로
But I'm swept up by you again
휩쓸려- swept up

끝나지 못한 이별 뒤
After a break up that can't end
끝나지 못한- can't be ended

이별과 이별 내게 남겨진 미련한 미련
Goodbye with goodbye the lasting reluctant reluctance
이별- separation; 미련- reluctance

널 잊지 못해 지우지 못해
I can't forget you, I can't erase you

눈에 담은 죄로
With eyes filled with wrong
담은- put in; 죄로- sin, crime, wrong

네 눈 속에 갇힌 나
I'm trapped in your eyes
갇힌- trapped

이토록 너는 아름다웠다
Like this you were beautiful.
이토록- like this

그토록 우린 행복했었다
Like this we were happy
행복했었다- were happy

너의 기억 속에서
In your memories

기억의 빛 속에서
In the light of the memories

난 살 수 있을 것만 같은데
Seems that I could just live

또 반복해낼 자신이 없어
But I don't think I can do this again
반복해낼- do again; 자신이- confidence

널 뚫고 나갈 자신이 없어
I don't think I can push through you and leave

네 사진 속에 난
I'm in your photo
사진- photo

그 눈 속에 비친 난
I'm reflected in those eyes

여전히 아무 것도 하지 못해
I still can't do anything
여전히- forever

울고 있잖아
So I'm crying
울다- to cry

너의 그 눈이 얼굴이
Your eyes, your face
얼굴- face

다시 나를 휘감아
They sweep me up again

창살처럼 넌 비로 내려와
Like raining prison bars you fall
창살- prison bars; -처럼- like

내 맘을 닫는다
Closing up my heart
닫다- to close

끝내지 못한 이별 뒤
After a break up that can't end
이별과 이별
Goodbye with goodbye
내게 남겨진 인연과 인연
The fate with fate that lasts with me

너를 벗어나려 해도
Even when I try to escape from you
멀리 도망치려 해도
Even when I try to run far away

또 휩쓸려 네게로
But I'm swept up by you again

끝나지 못한 이별 뒤
After a break up that can't end
이별과 이별
Goodbye with goodbye
내게 남겨진 미련한 미련
The fate with fate that lasts with me

널 잊지 못해 지우지 못해
I can't forget you, I can't erase you
눈에 담은 죄로
With eyes filled with wrong
네 눈 속에 갇힌 나
I'm trapped in your eyes
갇힌 나
Trapped

Red Velvet- Dumb Dumb

Lyrics/Translation/Notes

Dumb Dumb Dumb Dumb Dumb Dumb –
너 땜에 하루 종일 고민하지만
I'm thinking hard all day because of you
땜에- because of; 하루 종일- all day

널 어떡해야 좋을지 잘 모르겠어 난 Oh
But I still don't know what to do with you
~야- should; 잘- well, 모르겠어- wouldn't know

Baby baby baby baby baby You
Play me play me play me play me play me

그 눈빛은 날 아찔하고 헷갈리게 해
Your eyes take my breath away and confuse me
아찔하다- to amaze; 헷갈리다- to be confused

내 이성적인 감각들을 흩어지게 해 Oh
It makes my rational senses scatter away
이성적인- rational; 감각- sense; 흩어지게- scatter

Baby baby baby baby baby You
Crazy crazy crazy crazy crazy

마네킹 인형처럼
Like a mannequin,
마네킹- mannequin; 인형- appearance; ~처럼- like

하나부터 열까지 다 어색하지
everything is so awkward
하나- one; ~부터- from; 열- ten; ~까지- to; 다- all; 어색하다- to be awkward

평소같이 하면 되는데
I should just act like I do normally
평소- usual, normal; ~같이- like; 되는데- become okay

또 너만 보면 시작되는 바보 같은 춤
but whenever I see you, I act so stupid
시작- beginning; 바보- fool; 춤- dance

눈 코 입 표정도
My eyes, nose, lips,
표정- expression

팔 다리 걸음도
even my face, arms, legs, my walk,
팔- arm; 다리- leg; 걸음- step, walk

내 말을 듣지 않죠
they won't listen to me
듣지 않죠- won't listen; ~죠- (suggestive tag)

Dumb Dumb Dumb Dumb –

심장의 떨림도
The trembling of my heart,
심장의- heart's 떨림- beating

날 뛰는 기분도
my jumping moods,
뛰는- jumping; N+은/는- (adjective marker); 기분- mood, feeling

맘대로 되질 않죠
I can't control it
맘대로- according to one's self; 되질- become; 않죠- won't

Dumb Dumb Dumb Dumb –
Dumb Dumb Dumb Dumb Dumb Dumb –

낭만적인 영화를 난 꿈꿔왔지만
I've dreamed of a romantic movie
낭만적인- romantic; 영화- movie; 꿈꿔왔(지만)- dreamed (but)

네 사랑은 내 손에 늘 땀을 쥐게 해 Oh
But your love always makes my palms sweaty
사랑- love; 손에- in hand; 늘- always; 땀- sweat
Baby baby baby baby baby
You make me crazy crazy crazy crazy hey

마네킹 인형처럼
Like a mannequin,
하나부터 열까지 다 어색하지
everything is so awkward
평소같이 하면 되는데
I should just act like I do normally
또 너만 보면 시작되는 바보 같은 춤
but whenever I see you, I act so stupid
Dumb Dumb Dumb Dumb Dumb Dumb –

You need to "Beat It"
That boy Michael Jackson "Bad"
난 너의 "Billie Jean"이 아냐
I'm not your "Billie Jean"
Don't you "Leave Me Alone"
하지만 애매한 반응 난 원해 "Black or White"
But you're so ambiguous, I want "Black or White"
하지만- but; 애매한- unclear, ambiguous; 반응- reaction; 원해- want

포기 못해 나의 "Man in The Mirror"
I can't give up on you, my "Man in The Mirror"
포기- give up
"Why You Wanna Trip on Me"
넌 너무 짓궂지
You're too harsh
짓궂지- difficult, harsh
Boy, you make me "Scream"
너에게 왜 이러지
Why am I like this?
너에게- to you; 왜- why; 이러지- like this

하긴 너의 "Love 정말 Never Felt So Good"
Well, your "Love really Never Felt So Good"
하긴- well

그건 아마 짜릿하다 못해 Watching the "Thriller"
It's so electrifying that it's like watching the "Thriller"
아마- maybe; 짜릿하다- bright, electric

난 너에게서 헤어날 수 없나 봐
I can't escape from you
헤어나다- to separate, to escape

미워도 싫지가 않잖아
I hate you but I don't
미워- hatred; 싫지- truth

저 언니처럼 되고 싶은데
I wanna be like that unni
언니- older sister (used by younger females; 누나 is used by younger males)

넌 자꾸 나를 귀엽다고 하는 걸까 왜
But you keep calling me cute
자꾸- often; 귀엽다고- say cute

남동생 로봇처럼
Like my little brother's robot,
남동생- little brother

하나부터 열까지 다 어색하지 ha, ha, ha
everything is so awkward

어떡하지 고장 났나 봐
What do I do? I think I'm broken,
고장- breakdown, problem; 났나- occurred

숨을 쉬는 방법도 다 까먹었어 나
I forgot even how to breathe
숨- breath; 쉬는- breathed; 방법- method; 까먹었어- forgot

Dumb Dumb Dumb Dumb Dumb Dumb

눈 코 입 표정도
My eyes, nose, lips,
팔 다리 걸음도
even my face, arms, legs, my walk,
내 말을 듣지 않죠
they won't listen to me
Dumb Dumb Dumb Dumb –
심장의 떨림도
The trembling of my heart,
날뛰는 기분도
my jumping moods,
맘대로 되질 않죠
I can't control it

Dumb Dumb Dumb Dumb –

Dumb Dumb Dumb Dumb Dumb Dumb –
(Baby~, do~, I must be, oh~)

Girls Generation- I Got a Boy

Tiffany, Sunny, Taeyeon, Yuri, Yoona, Seolhyun, Jessica, Hyoyeon, Sooyoung

Lyrics/Translation/Notes

Ayo! GG!
Yeah Yeah
시작해 볼까?
Shall we start?
~까- (suggestive ending)

어머!
Oh my!

얘 좀 봐라 얘, 무슨 일이 있었길래 머릴 잘랐대? 응?
Look at her, what made her cut her hair? Huh?
얘- her (casual form); ~라- (suggestive or command ending); 무슨- what; 일이-
occurrence
어머!
Oh my!
또 얘 좀 보라고!
Look at her again!
머리부터 발끝까지 스타일이 바뀌었어.
A changed style from head to toe.
머리- head; ~부터- from; ~까지- to; 발- foot; 끝- end; 바뀌었- changed, replaced
왜 그랬대?
Why did she do that?

89

궁금해 죽겠네 왜 그랬대?
I'm dying of curiosity! Why did she do that?
궁금- concern; 죽겠네- dying(slang)

말해 봐봐 좀. Why?
Please tell me. Why?

Ha ha ha
Hey let me introduce myself!
Here comes trouble!
따라 해!
Follow me!

Oh, oh oh eh oh, oh oh eh oh oh oh

너 잘났어 정말!
You're getting overconfident, really!
잘났어- well turned out, prideful; 정말- really

지가 뭔데? 웃겨!
Who does she think she is? Ridiculous!

너무 콧대 센 거 아니?
Wasn't that a little too arrogant?
콧대- arrogant; 센- strong

나보고 평범하단다, 얘.
Telling me that I'm ordinary, eh.
나보고- seeing me and; 평범한- average, ordinary; 단다- say, tell

그 남자 완전 맘에 들었나 봐!
So, she's totally in love with that boy!
완전- complete, total; 맘에 들어- matches my mind

말도 안돼! 말도 안돼!
Ridiculous! Ridiculous!
말도 안돼- speechless, senseless, ~도- even

너무 예뻐지고 섹시해 졌어 그 남자 때문이지?
She became pretty and sexy all for that man?
예뻐지고- pretty and; 때문- because

물어볼 뻔 했다니까~ 너 바꾼 화장품이 뭔지?
Because I almost asked her- "Which cosmetic products are you using right now?"
~을 뻔- almost; 했다- did, ~니까- because, since; 화장품- cosmetics

사실 나, 처음 봤어 상처 입은 야수 같은 깊은 눈.
Honestly, I saw it for the first time, the eyes that look like those of a wounded animal's.

상처- wound; 입은 - has, wearing; 야수- wild animal; 같은- like, similar to
얘기만 해도 어질 했다니까?
I told you I felt dizzy just by talking to you?
얘기- talk; ~만- only; 어지럽다- to be dizzy

너 잘났어 정말! 잘났어 정말!
You're getting overconfident, really!
정말- really, truly

Oh
Here comes trouble!
Oh oh eh oh
Hey girl listen!
Oh oh eh oh oh oh

너 잘났다.
You're getting overconfident.
잘났서.
Overconfident.

Oh, oh oh eh oh, oh oh eh oh oh oh

너 잘났어, 정말!
You're getting overconfident, really!

Ayo! Stop!
Let me put it down another way

I got a boy 멋진! I got a boy 착한!
I got a boy, he's awesome! I got a boy, he's kind!
I got a boy handsome boy 내 맘 다 가져간
I got a boy, handsome boy, my heart got taken away
I got a boy 멋진! I got a boy 착한!
I got a boy, he's awesome! I got a boy, he's kind!

I got a boy awesome boy 완전 반했나 봐
I got a boy, awesome boy, I guess I've completely fallen for you.
반하다- to fall in love

아 내 왕자님!
Ah, my prince!
언제 이 몸을 구하러 와 주실 텐가요?
When are you going to rescue this body of mine?
구하(러)- save (in order to); 텐- would

하얀 꿈처럼.
Like white dreams.
날 품에 안아 올려 날아가 주시겠죠?
Will you be embracing me and taking me to the sky?
품- bosom

나, 깜짝! 멘붕이야!
I'm shocked! A mental breakdown!
그 사람은 내 민 낯이 궁금하대.
That person is curious about my face.
민 낯이- no makeup face
완전 맘에 들어 못 이긴 척.
I like him a lot.
보여줘도 괜찮을까?
Will it be alright to show him?
괜찮아- okay, good, satisfactory
오우! 절대로 안되지!
Oh! Absolutely not!
절대로- absolutely
그치? 그치?
Isn't that right? Isn't that right?
우리, 지킬 건 지키자!
We have to guard what we have to guard!
지키다- to protect, guard
맞지! 맞지!
That's right! That's right!

그의 맘을 모두 가질 때까지이건 절대로 잊어버리지 말라고!
Don't forget this until the day you own all of his heart!
가지다- to take; 절대로- absolutely; 잊어버리다- to forget

Oh, oh oh eh oh, oh oh eh oh oh oh

밤을 새도 모자라 다 다.
Even if I stay up all night, everything is not enough.
밤을 새도- to stay up all night; 모자리다- not enough
Oh, oh oh eh oh, oh oh eh oh

우리 최고 관심사 다 다.
Our biggest interest, everything, everything.
최고- biggest, favorite; 관심사- person of interest

내 말 들어봐 그 아이 너네 알지?
Listen to me, you know that kid, right?
그 아이- that kid; 너네- you guys

좀 어리지만 속은 꽉 찼어.
He's young but his mind is full.
어리다- to be young

어떨 땐 오빠처럼 듬직하지만.
Even though he's like a dependable oppa sometimes.
어떨 땐- sometimes; 듬직한- dependable

애교를 부릴 땐 너무 예뻐 죽겠어.
He's extremely adorable when he does his aegyo.
죽겠어- would die

Oh, oh oh eh oh, oh oh eh oh oh

너 미쳤어, 미쳤어.
You're crazy, crazy.
Oh, oh oh eh oh, oh oh eh oh
너 미쳤어, 미쳤어.
You're crazy, crazy.

난 정말 화가 나 죽겠어.
I'm seriously frustrated.
화- anger, frustration

내 남잔 날 여자로 안보는 걸.
My man doesn't treat me like a girl.
안보는 걸- not see a thing

막연할 땐 어떡하면 내가 좋겠니?
What should I do when I'm uncertain like this?
막연- loose, uncertain; 땐- time, period

질투라도 나게 해볼까? 속상해! 어떡해! 나?
Should I try making him jealous? It's so aggravating! What should I do?
질투- jealousy; 속상하다- to be frustrating, aggravating

말도 안 돼! 말도 안 돼!
Ridiculous! Ridiculous!

Don't stop! Let's bring it back to 140.

I got a boy 멋진! I got a boy 착한!
I got a boy, he's awesome! I got a boy, he's kind!

I got a boy handsome boy 내 맘 다 가져간
I got a boy, handsome boy, my heart got taken away
I got a boy 멋진! I got a boy 착한!
I got a boy, he's awesome! I got a boy, he's kind!
I got a boy awesome boy 완전 반했나 봐.
I got a boy, awesome boy, I guess I've completely fallen for you

언제나 내 곁엔 내편이 돼주고 귀 기울여주는 너— 너—.
The one who has always been with me, right by my side, lending me a listening ear, it was you, you.
곁엔/곁에는- side; 편- side; 귀- ear; 기울여주는- lend (lit. giving tilt)

No oh oh oh oh

난 이대로 지금 행복해.
I'm happy like this.

잘 될 거니까.
Because things are going to get better now.

I got a boy 멋진! I got a boy 착한!
I got a boy, he's awesome! I got a boy, he's kind!
아 내 왕자님!
Ah, my prince!
I got a boy handsome boy 내 맘 다 가져간.
I got a boy, handsome boy, my heart got taken away
언제 이 몸을 구하러 와 주실 텐가요?
When are you going to rescue this body of mine?
I got a boy 멋진! I got a boy 착한!
I got a boy, he's awesome! I got a boy, he's kind!
하얀 꿈처럼.
Like white dreams.

I got a boy awesome boy 완전 반했나 봐.
I got a boy, awesome boy, I guess I've completely fallen for you.
날 품에 안아 올려 날아가 주시겠죠?
Will you be embracing me and taking me to the sky?
I got a boy 멋진! I got a boy 착한!
I got a boy, he's awesome! I got a boy, he's kind!

Oh oh oh eh oh, oh oh eh oh
I got a boy handsome boy 내 맘 다 가져간.
I got a boy, handsome boy, my heart got taken away.

Oh oh oh eh oh, oh oh eh oh
I got a boy 멋진! I got a boy 착한!
I got a boy, he's awesome! I got a boy, he's kind!

Oh oh oh eh oh, oh oh eh oh

I got a boy 멋진!
I got a boy, he's awesome!

Girls Generation- Gee

Lyrics/Translation/Notes

Uh Huh Listen Boy
Aha! Listen Boy
My First Love Story
My Angel & My Girls
My Sunshine Uh Uh Let's go

너무 너무 멋져 눈이 눈이 부셔.
You're so, so handsome, I'm blinded.
너무- too much; 멋져- cool, handsome; 눈- eye; 부셔- blinded
숨을 못 쉬겠어 떨리는걸.
I can't breathe because I'm trembling.
숨- breath; 쉬(겠)어- breathe (I think); 떨리는- trembling

Gee Gee Gee Gee Baby Baby Baby
Gee Gee Gee Gee Baby Baby Baby

oh 너무 부끄러워 쳐다 볼 수 없어.
Oh I feel so embarrassed, I can't look at you.
부끄러워- embarrassed; 쳐다 볼 (수 없어)- look(can't)
사랑에 빠져서 수줍은걸.
I feel shy because I've fallen in love.
빠져서- fallen; 수줍은- shy

Gee Gee Gee Gee Baby Baby Baby

Gee Gee Gee Gee Be Be Be Be Be Be
(어떻게 하죠) 어떡 어떡하죠.
(What should I do?) What should I do?
어떡하(죠)- how(?)
(떨리는 나는) 떨리는 나는요.
(About my trembling heart) My trembling heart.
떨리는- trembling

(두근 두근 두근 두근)
(Thump thump thump thump)
두근 두근거려
My heart kept thumping
밤엔 잠도 못 이루죠.
so, I couldn't fall asleep at night.
이루죠- make happen
나는 나는 바본가봐요.
I guess I guess I'm a fool.
바본가봐요)- foolish(appear)
그대 그대밖에 모르는 바보.
A fool that knows nothing except you.
그대밖에- you(except)
그래요 그댈 보는 난.
Yes, as I look at you.
그래요- indeed, like that

너무 반짝 반짝 눈이 부셔.
So bright my eyes are blinded.
반짝 반짝- shimmering
No No No No No
너무 깜짝 깜짝 놀란 나는.
So surprised surprised, I'm shocked.
깜짝 깜짝- surprising
Oh Oh Oh Oh Oh
너무 짜릿 짜릿 몸이 떨려.
So tingly tingly, my body is trembling.
짜릿 짜릿- trembling
Gee Gee Gee Gee Gee
Oh 젖은 눈빛. Oh yeah.
Oh glittering eyes. Oh yeah.
젖은- soaked, filled

Oh 좋은 향기. Oh yeah yeah yeah.
Oh sweet aroma. Oh yeah yeah yeah.
향기- perfume

Oh 너무 너무 예뻐 맘이 너무 예뻐.
Oh so pretty, your heart is so pretty.
예뻐- pretty

첫 눈에 반했어 꼭 짚은 걸.
I was captured from the first glance.
첫- first; 눈에- eye(to); 반했어- fallen, captured

Gee Gee Gee Gee Baby Baby Baby
Gee Gee Gee Gee Baby Baby Baby

너무나 뜨거워 만질 수가 없어.
I can't touch it because it's so hot.
너무(나)- too much(too). 나 is emphatic.; 뜨거워- hot; 만질 (수가 없어)- touch(can't)

사랑에 타버려 후끈한걸.
I'm engulfed by love's fire completely.
타버려- burned; 후끈한걸- hit, engulfed

Gee Gee Gee Gee Baby Baby Baby
Gee Gee Gee Gee Be Be Be Be Be Be

(어쩌면 좋아) 어쩌면 좋아요?
(What should I do?) What should I do?
어쩌면- how(if)

(수줍은 나는) 수줍은 나는요.
(Because I'm so shy) I am so shy.

(몰라 몰라 몰라 몰라).
(I don't know, I don't know).

몰라 몰라 하며.
I don't know why.

[매일 그대만 그리죠.
Every day I long for only you.
그리죠- miss

친한 친구들은 말하죠.
My close friends tell me,
친한- friendly

정말 너는 정말 못말려 바보.
that I'm really a helpless fool.

못말려- stop; 바보- fool; 못말려 바보- can't stop being a fool

하지만 그댈 보는 난...
But as I look at you...
하지만- but

너무 반짝 반짝 눈이 부셔.
So bright my eyes are blinded.
No No No No No
너무 깜짝 깜짝 놀란 나는.
So surprised surprised, I'm shocked.
Oh Oh Oh Oh Oh
너무 짜릿 짜릿 몸이 떨려.
So tingly tingly, my body is trembling.
Gee Gee Gee Gee Gee
Oh 젖은 눈빛. Oh yeah.
Oh glittering eyes. Oh yeah.
Oh 좋은 향기. Oh yeah yeah yeah.
Oh sweet aroma. Oh yeah yeah yeah.

말도 못했는 걸.
I can't even say anything.
너무 부끄러워 하는 난.
I'm too embarrassed.
용기가 없는 걸까.
Do I not have any courage?.
용기- courage, bravery
어떡해야 좋은 걸까?
What would be the right thing to do?
어떡해(야)- how(should)
두근두근 맘 졸이며.
Pit-a-pat my heart is anxious as
졸이(며)- anxious(as)
바라보고 있는 난.
I'm looking at you.
바라보고- staring at, gazing at

너무 반짝 반짝 눈이 부셔.
So bright my eyes are blinded.
No No No No No
너무 깜짝 깜짝 놀란 나는.
So surprised surprised, I'm shocked.

Oh Oh Oh Oh Oh

너무 짜릿 짜릿 몸이 떨려.
So tingly tingly, my body is trembling.
Gee Gee Gee Gee Gee
Oh 젖은 눈빛. Oh yeah.
Oh glittering eyes. Oh yeah.
Oh 좋은 향기. Oh yeah yeah yeah.
Oh sweet aroma. Oh yeah yeah yeah.

너무 반짝 반짝 눈이 부셔.
So bright my eyes are blinded.
No No No No No
너무 깜짝 깜짝 놀란 나는.
So surprised surprised, I'm shocked.
Oh Oh Oh Oh Oh
너무 짜릿 짜릿 몸이 떨려.
So tingly tingly, my body is trembling.
Gee Gee Gee Gee Gee
Oh 젖은 눈빛. Oh yeah.
Oh glittering eyes. Oh yeah.
Oh 좋은 향기. Oh yeah yeah yeah.
Oh sweet aroma. Oh yeah yeah yeah.

Big Bang- Loser

GDragon, Top, Taeyang, Daesung, Seungri

Lyrics/Translation/Notes

Loser 외톨이 센 척하는 겁쟁이
Loser, loner, a coward who pretends to be tough
외톨이- loner; 센- firmly; 척하는- pretending; 겁쟁이- coward

못된 양아치 거울 속에 넌
A mean delinquent, in the mirror, you're
못된- badly turned out; 거울- mirror, 속에 - in

Just a loser 외톨이 상처뿐인 머저리
Just a loser, a loner, a jackass covered in scars
상처- wound, scar; 머저리- punk, jackass

더러운 쓰레기 거울 속에 난 I'm a
Dirty trash, in the mirror, I'm a
~운- adjective marker; 더러운- dirty, ~운- adjective

솔직히 세상과 난 어울린 적 없어
Honestly, I've never fit in with the world
솔직히- honestly, candidly; ~히- adverb marker; 어울린- matching

홀로였던 내겐 사랑 따윈 벌써 잊혀진지
I was always alone, I've forgotten about love
홀로- loneliness; 따윈- kind of, type of, such as it is

오래 저 시간 속에
It's been a long time since
오래- long time

더 이상은 못 듣겠어 희망찬 사랑 노래
I can't listen to hopeful love songs anymore
희망- hope, ambition; 희망차다- to expect a lot.

너나 나나 그저 길들여진 대로
You and me both
길들이다- to tame; 대로- as

각본 속에 놀아나는 슬픈 삐에로
We're just sad clowns, tamed and scripted
각본- script; 삐에로- clown

난 멀리 와버렸어 I'm coming home
I've come far and wasted , I'm coming home
멀리- far

이제 다시 돌아갈래 어릴 적 제자리로
I wanna go back to when I was young
돌아갈래- return; 어릴 적- childish side; 제자리(로)-original place(to)

언제부턴가 난
At some point, I started looking
언제부턴가- from some time

하늘 보다 땅을 더 바라보게 돼
At the ground, more than the sky
땅- ground, dirt; 바라보다- stare; 돼 - became

숨쉬기조차 힘겨워
It's hard even to breathe
숨쉬다- breath

손을 뻗지만 그 누구도
I hold out my hand to whomever even
뻗지만- hold out but; 누구- who

날 잡아 주질 않네 I'm a
But no one holds it, I'm a
잡아- grab, hold

Loser 외톨이 센 척하는 겁쟁이
Loser, loner, a coward who pretends to be tough
못된 양아치 거울 속에 넌
A mean delinquent, in the mirror, you're
못된- bad result

Just a loser 외톨이 상처뿐인 머저리
Just a loser, a loner, a jackass covered in scars
더러운 쓰레기 거울 속에 난 I'm a
Dirty trash, in the mirror, I'm a

반복되는 여자들과의 내 실수
It's a cycle of girls and mistakes
반복- repeat; 실수 - mistake
하룻밤을 사랑하고 해 뜨면 싫증
If I ove them for one night- disgust
싫증- disgust
책임지지 못 할 나의 이기적인 기쁨
I can't own up to it, because of my selfish pleasure
책임- responsibility; 지지- support, 못 할- can't; 이기적인- selfish, egotistical

하나 땜에 모든 것이 망가져버린 지금
Now, because of one thing everything is being ruined
망하 - to ruin; 가져- bring; 버리다- throw away
멈출 줄 모르던 나의 위험한 질주
I can't stop this dangerous run
멈출- stop; 줄- way; 위험한- dangerous; 질주- stride, run
이젠 아무런 감흥도 재미도 없는 기분
Now I have no interest, no fun anymore
아무런- any, whatever; 감흥- interest; 기분- frame of mind, mood
나 벼랑 끝에 혼자 있네 I'm going home
I'm alone at the edge of a cliff, I'm going home
벼랑- cliff
나 다시 돌아갈래 예전의 제자리로
I wanna go back, to how it was before
예전- before; 제자리- right place
언제부턴가 난
At some point, I've
사람들의 시선을 두려워만 해
Gotten scared of people's eyes
시선을- sight; 두려워만- only fear

우는 것조차 지겨워 웃어보지만
I'm sick of even crying so I tried smiling but
지겨워- bored, tired of

그 아무도 날 알아주질 않네 I'm a
no one recognizes me, I'm a
알아주질- gives recognition

Loser 외톨이 센 척하는 겁쟁이
Loser, loner, a coward who pretends to be tough
못된 양아치 거울 속에 넌
A mean delinquent, in the mirror, you're
Just a loser 외톨이 상처뿐인 머저리
Just a loser, a loner, a jackass covered in scars
더러운 쓰레기 거울 속에 난 I'm a
Dirty trash, in the mirror, I'm a

파란 저 하늘을 원망하지 난
I curse the blue skies
파란- blue; 저- that; 원망하지- curse, cry out at

가끔 내려놓고 싶어져
Sometimes I wanna lay it all down
내려놓고- put down and

I wanna say good bye

이 길의 끝에 방황이 끝나면
When I stop wandering at the end of this road
길의- streets; 방황- wandering

부디 후회 없는 채로 두 눈 감을 수 있길
I hope I can close my eyes without regrets
부디- hopefully, please; 후회 없는- without regret; 채로- in that way; ~길/길래-
(suggestive of speaker's desire)

Loser 외톨이 센 척하는 겁쟁이
Loser, loner, a coward who pretends to be tough
못된 양아치 거울 속에 넌
A mean delinquent, in the mirror, you're
Just a loser 외톨이 상처뿐인 머저리
Just a loser, a loner, a jackass covered in scars
Loser, oh

더러운 쓰레기 거울 속에 난 I'm a
Dirty trash, in the mirror, I'm a
Loser
I'm a loser
I'm a loser
I'm a loser

Big Bang- Fantastic Baby

Lyrics/Translation/Notes

여기 붙어라 모두 모여라
Come together, everyone gather here
붙어라- call, sing; 모여라- gather; V+라- (suggestion or command tag)
<u>We gon' part like</u>

<u>lilililalala</u>

맘을 열어라 머릴 비워라
Open your hearts, empty your minds
열어라- open; 머리- head, mind; 비워라- empty
불을 지펴라
Set the fire

<u>lilililalala</u>

정답은 묻지 말고 그대로 받아들여
Don't ask for the answer but just take it as it is
정답- right answer; 묻지 말(고)- don't ask (and); 그대로- as it is
<u>느낌대로 가</u> alright
Go with the flow alright
느낌대로- as feeling

하늘을 마주하고 두 손을 다 위로
Face the sky and put your two hands up, up high
마주(하고)- face(and); 두- two; 위(로)- up(toward)

저 위로 날뛰고 싶어 oh
Wanna jump around oh
날뛰고- rampage
nanananana

Wow fantastic baby

Dance
I wanna dan dan dan dan dance

Fantastic baby

Dance
I wanna dan dan dan dan dance

Wow fantastic baby

이 난장판에 hey
In this crazy house, hey
난장판- mess

끝판 왕 차례 hey
At the end, it's the king's turn hey
왕- king; 차례- turn

땅을 흔들고
The ground is shaking and
흔들리다- to shake

3 분으론 불충분한
3 minutes is not enough for this
불충분한- not enough
race wait

분위기는 과열 huh
The atmosphere is overheated huh
과열- overheated
Catch me on fire huh

진짜가 나타났다 나나나나
The real has appeared nananana
진짜- truth

하나부터 열까지 모든 게 다 한 수위
From one to ten, everything is one level above
수위- level up

모래 벌판 위를 미친 듯이
Act like we crazily run on sand
모래 벌판- sand field; 듯이- as if, meaning

뛰어봐도 거뜬한 우리
We're still so agile
거뜬한- light, agile

하늘은 충분히 너무나 푸르니까
Because the sky is blue enough
충분히- enough; 푸르(니까)- blue(because)

아무것도 묻지 말란 말이야
Don't ask any questions, just feel it
아무것도- Even anything

느끼란 말이야 내가 누군지
With feeling I say, who am I?
느끼란- with feeling

네 심장소리에 맞게 뛰기 시작해
Jump at the sound of your heartbeat
심장소리에- at the sound of heart; 맞게- matching

막이 끝날 때까지 ye
'Till this comes to an end yeah
막이- the end, the close; 때까지- until the time

I can't baby don't stop this

오늘은 타락해
Just go corrupt today
미쳐 발악해
Go crazy and rave
가는거야
Let's go

Wow fantastic baby

Dance
I wanna dan dan dan dan dance

Fantastic baby

Dance
I wanna dan dan dan dan dance

Wow fantastic baby
Boom shakalaka
Boom shakalaka
Boom shakalaka
dan dan dan dan dance

Boom shakalaka
Boom shakalaka
Boom shakalaka

dan dan dan dan

날 따라 잡아볼 테면 와봐
Catch me if you can
난 영원한 딴따라
I'm forever outrageous
딴따라- outrageously, outrageous
오늘 밤 금기란 내겐 없어
There are no constraints for me tonight
금기- prohibition, constraint
Mama just let me be your lover

이 혼란 속을 넘어
Past this chaos
혼란- mess, chaos, confusion
nanananana

머리끝부터 발끝까지 비쥬얼은 쇼크
From my head to my toes, there's a visual shock
비쥬얼- visual; 쇼크- shock
내 감각은 소문난 꾼 앞서가는 촉
People know me for my senses that are
always ahead
감각- sense; 소문난- famous 꾼- players; 촉- point

남들보다는 빠른 걸음
My footsteps are faster than others
빠른 걸음- fast steps
차원이 다른 젊음
My youth is a different dimension
차원- dimension

얼음얼음얼음
Ice ice ice

Hold up
nanananana

네 심장소리에 맞게 뛰기 시작해
Jump at the sound of your heartbeat
막이 끝날 때까지 yeah
Till this comes to an end yeah

I can't baby don't stop this
오늘은 타락해
Just go corrupt today
미쳐 발악해
Go crazy and rave
가는거야
Let's go

Wow fantastic baby

Dance
I wanna dan dan dan dan dance

Fantastic baby

Dance
I wanna dan dan dan dan dance

Wow fantastic baby

Boom shakalaka
Boom shakalaka
Boom shakalaka

dan dan dan dan dance

Boom shakalaka
Boom shakalaka
Boom shakalaka

dan dan dan dan

다 같이 놀자
Let's all play together

Yeah yeah yeah

다 같이 뛰자
Let's all jump together

Yeah yeah yeah

다 같이 돌자
Let's all go crazy together

Yeah yeah yeah

다 같이 가자
Let's all go together

Wow fantastic baby

Big Bang- Bang, Bang, Bang

Lyrics/Translation/Notes

난 깨어나 까만 밤과 함께
I awake with the black night
깨어나- wake; 까만- black; 함께- together

다 들어와 담엔 누구 차례
Everyone come in, who's turn is it next?
들어와- come in; 담엔/다음에- next

한 치 앞도 볼 수 없는 막장 게릴라
Can't see an inch forward, crazy guerilla
한 치- one inch; 막장- crazy, ridiculous

경배하라 목청이 터지게
Worship, exploding scream
경배하라- do worship; 터지게- exploding

찌질한 분위기를 전환해
Switch up this loser atmosphere
찌질한- nerdy, loser; 분위기- surroundings

광기를 감추지 못하게 해
So the insanity can not be hid
광기- madness, insanity; 감추지- hide

남자들의 품위 여자들의 가식
The dignity of men, the pretense of women
품위- class, dignity; 가식- pretense

이유 모를 자신감이 볼만해
Just look at this unreasonable confidence
자신감- confidence; 이유- reason

난 보란 듯이 너무나도 뻔뻔히
As if I'm showing off so brazenly
뻔뻔히- brazen, shameless

니 몸속에 파고드는 알러지
I dig into your body like an allergy
파고드는- digging

이상한 정신의 술렁이는 천지
The strange mind's roaring world
술렁이는 천지- roaring world

오늘 여기 무법지
Today, this place is lawless
무법- lawless

난 불을 질러
I scream fire
질러- shout

심장을 태워
Burn up your heart
심장- heart

널 미치게 하고 싶어
I wanna make you go crazy
미치게- crazy
B.I.G yea we bang like this

모두 다 같이
Everyone together

총 맞은 것처럼
Like being shot
총- gun; 맞은- shot, hit

Bang! Bang! Bang!
Bang! Bang! Bang!

빵야 빵야 빵야
bang bang bang

Bang! Bang! Bang!
Bang! Bang! Bang!
빵야 빵야 빵야
bang bang bang

다 꼼짝 마라 다 꼼짝 마
Nobody move, nobody move
다 꼼짝 마라 다 꼼짝 마
Nobody move, nobody move
오늘 밤 끝장 보자 다 끝장 봐
Let's see the end of this night, see the end of all
끝장- end of a thing
오늘 밤 끝장 보자
Let's see the end of this night

빵야 빵야 빵야
Bang bang bang

널 데려가 지금 이 순간에
I'll take you away now at this moment
데려가- take; give a ride; 순간- moment
새빨간 저 하늘이 춤출 때
When that scarlet sky dances
새빨간- bright red; 춤출- will dance; 때- when; at that time
돌고 돌아 너와 나 이곳은 Valhalla
Spinning and spinning, you and I, this place is Valhalla
돌다- to turn, spin
찬양하라 더 울려 퍼지게
Give praise and spread it out louder
찬양- praise; 퍼지게- diffusively
We go hard 불침번
We go hard, night watchmen

밤새 달려 축지법
Run all night with space magic
밤새- all night; 축지법- magic art of shortening space
이 노래는 꼭지점 신이나 불러라 신점
This song is the apex, call the spirit
꼭지점- apex, top; 신- spirit; 신점- spirit spot
큰 비명소리는 마성의 멜로디
Loud screams are devilish melodies

마성- devilish

검은 독기의 연결 고리
Ring connection to a black poison
독- poison; 연결- connection; 고리- ring (sound)
사방 팔방 오방 가서 푸는 고삐 whoo
All around you, get high and release the reins whoo
사방/팔방- all directions; 오방- south, direction of the horse

난 불을 질러
I scream fire
네 심장을 태워
Burn up your heart
널 미치게 하고 싶어
I wanna make you go crazy

B.I.G yea we bang like this

모두 다 같이
Everyone together

총 맞은 것처럼
Like being shot

Bang! Bang! Bang!
Bang! Bang! Bang!

빵야 빵야 빵야
bang bang bang

Bang! Bang! Bang!
Bang! Bang! Bang!

빵야 빵야 빵야
bang bang bang

다 꼼짝 마라 다 꼼짝 마
Nobody move, nobody move
다 꼼짝 마라 다 꼼짝 마
Nobody move, nobody move
오늘 밤 끝장 보자 다 끝장 봐
Let's see the end of this night, see the end
오늘 밤 끝장 보자
Let's see the end of this night

빵야 빵야 빵야
Bang bang bang

Ready or not
Yea we don't give a what
Ready or not
Yea we don't give a what
Let's go 남자들은 위로
Let's go, guys go on top
여자들은 get low
Girls get low
당겨라 bang bang bang
Pull the trigger, bang bang bang

Let the bass drum go

남자들은 위로
Guys go on top
여자들은 get low
Girls get low
당겨라 bang bang bang
Pull the trigger, bang bang bang

Let the bass drum go

Ehh

Let the bass drum go

Ehh

Bang bang bang

Ehh

Bang bang bang

Ehh

Bang bang bang

Ehh

Bang bang bang

Ehh

Let the bass drum go

Other recommended books to help you learn Korean with popular Korean culture:

Learn Korean thru K-pop
Learn Korean with Big Bang
Learn Korean with Girls' Generation
Learn Korean with Korean Drama: The Heirs Episode 1

All available on Amazon.com thru Createspace Publishing

Have any ideas or want something to help you learn Korean that is not currently available? The author is glad to read your suggestions. Contact Peter Kang at **kimchimanus@gmail.com**.

Printed in Great Britain
by Amazon